To Bob & Lou,

MICHAEL DUFFY

CALL ME CRUEL

A story about murder and the
dangerous power of lies

Michael Duffy

ALLEN&UNWIN

SYDNEY • MELBOURNE • AUCKLAND • LONDON

First published in 2012
Copyright © Michael Duffy 2012

Allen & Unwin
Sydney, Melbourne, Auckland, London
83 Alexander Street
Crows Nest NSW 2065
Australia
Phone: (61 2) 8425 0100
Fax: (61 2) 9906 2218
Email: info@allenandunwin.com
Web: www.allenandunwin.com

Cataloguing-in-Publication details are available
from the National Library of Australia
www.trove.nla.gov.au

ISBN 978 1 74237 269 3

Map by Ian Faulkner

Set in 12.5/17 pt Bembo by Post Pre-press Group, Australia
Printed and bound in Australia by Griffin Press

10 9 8 7 6 5 4 3 2 1

The paper in this book is FSC® certified.
FSC® promotes environmentally responsible,
socially beneficial and economically viable
management of the world's forests.

Michael Duffy reports trials and crime for the *Sun-Herald*. He has written two Sydney crime novels, *The Tower* and *The Simple Death*.

www.michaelduffy.com.au

i.m. Kylie Labouchardiere (née Edwards)
(1980–2004)

CONTENTS

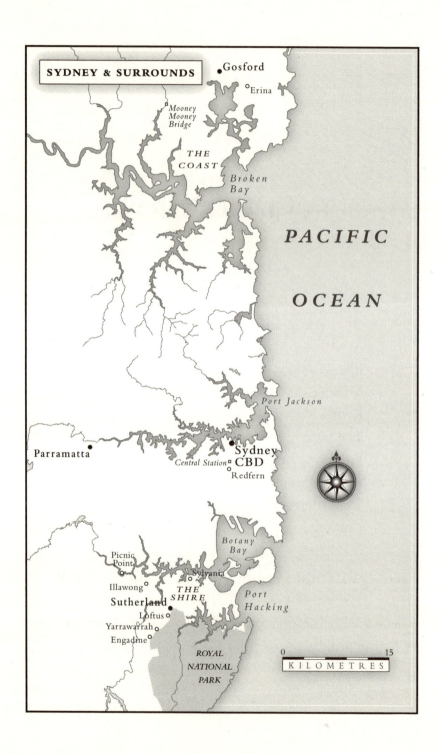

SYDNEY & SURROUNDS

Gosford

Erina

Mooney
Mooney
Bridge

*THE
COAST*

*Broken
Bay*

PACIFIC

OCEAN

Port Jackson

Parramatta

**Sydney
CBD**

Central Station

Redfern

*Botany
Bay*

Picnic
Point

Sylvania

Illawong

*THE
SHIRE*

*Port
Hacking*

Sutherland

Loftus

Yarrawarrah

Engadine

*ROYAL
NATIONAL
PARK*

0   15

K I L O M E T R E S

INTRODUCTION

When I began to attend murder trials as a journalist, I was curious to find out how real murder differed from fiction. Like most people, I was fortunate that my only knowledge of violent death came from crime novels and television dramas. I knew reality would be different, but how?

I found many differences, but the main one was the character of the murderer. In fiction, killers are often psychopaths who plan their crimes, have multiple victims and are adept at avoiding capture, sometimes even taunting their pursuers. These characteristics satisfy the need to personify evil, for greater dramatic and moral effect.

Most of the murderers I've seen in the dock are not like this. In real life, murder often involves an action committed on the spur of a moment created by unusual circumstances. Because of their lack of experience and intent, most killers are caught fairly easily and often plead guilty. They are very different to the psychopaths and gangsters of fiction, tending to be either mildly unstable individuals or relatively normal people who did something terrible but might easily not have. Although killers receive some of the longest sentences going, most are among the least criminally inclined of jail inmates. Many deeply regret their crimes.

Paul Wilkinson is different. He was an Aboriginal Community Liaison Officer with the police force and used his special knowledge to help him kill and evade arrest for years afterwards. His most striking behaviour, before and after he strangled Kylie Labouchardiere, was a propensity to tell massive and complex lies, which those around him believed. He was charming and persuasive, yet some of his lies were so bizarre—essentially, he turned his own life into a work of fiction—that one of the most curious aspects of this story is that it took so long to catch him. The investigation lasted three years and, even after he was locked up and examined by psychiatrists, he was never declared insane.

Wilkinson's lies fooled his wife, Julie, into moving out of their home so he could conduct an affair. They lured twenty-three-year-old Kylie Labouchardiere away from her husband. Like most good liars, he was clever at identifying gullible people and getting close to them—in Kylie's case, partly through the exchange of an extraordinary 23,000 text messages over four months. But finally he fooled himself too, and his lies blossomed into complex fantasies he no longer controlled. They came to control him, and in the end they drove him to murder. This is a story about the power of stories, about what can happen when we lose the ability to tell the difference between fact and fiction.

One way to lose touch with reality is to stop feeling anything for other people. Paul Wilkinson has never revealed where Kylie is buried. This book's title is taken from a chilling text message he sent his wife during the police investigation:

'Everybody has reasons 4 hiding a crime. Mine is the family can live not knowing where and why 4 What they hav don. Call me cruel, call me nasty and YES Id agree, howeva my knowledge ISNT goin 2 b theres. It will hurt them NOT me.'

Just what did he mean by that? Obviously he was being cruel, and knew his actions appeared cruel. But did he actually have any feeling for the misery he was causing Kylie's family? Whatever the answer to that question, a layperson might well feel that the man who sent that text was crazy. Yet after his arrest he was examined several times by several psychiatrists, who found he was responsible for his actions.

Another major difference between real murder and fiction lies with the victim. In reality, victims are often men and know their killer. In fiction, they tend to be young women or even children, often selected almost at random. Just as fiction exaggerates the evil of the murderer, it heightens the weakness and innocence of his prey.

Kylie Labouchardiere was a vulnerable young woman, but it was more complicated than that. Some terrible things had happened in her life, and because of her character these had been even more devastating than they might have been for most women. Her sister, Leanne, says that as Kylie was growing up it became obvious she was drawn to dangerous situations: 'alarm bells just didn't ring for her'. Tragically, she never grew out of this behaviour.

The word 'tragedy' does not only mean something awful or horrific. It can also mean a personal disaster that occurs partly because of a flaw in an individual's character. This does not mean that victims deserve what happens to them; it is simply an acknowledgement that some people, due to a combination of character, upbringing and circumstances, are more likely than others to be victims. This sad truth is on display in Australia's courts every working day, a reminder of the enormous role luck plays in all our lives.

Kylie Labouchardiere's death was a tragedy, in the full sense of the word. It was terribly unlucky that Paul Wilkinson should kill and that she should die. But in retrospect, I believe we can see that if Wilkinson was ever going to kill, his victim was going to be someone like Kylie. It would be someone prepared to enter his weird fictional world—someone who didn't hear the alarm bells.

This makes her sound gullible, and in some ways she was. But in many ways, so too was the justice system, which took five long years to convict Paul Wilkinson, despite the fact that the police strongly suspected him almost from the start. The institutions we have created to protect society— the police force and the courts—had great trouble dealing with Wilkinson. The individuals involved often knew he was taking them for a ride, but because of the rules—and Wilkinson's capacity to abuse those rules—they were unable to do anything about it, which extended the period during which he was able to hurt people.

Indeed, one of the most disturbing things about this story is not only that he left a trail of broken careers and marriages and lives in his wake—a trail of misery and devastation—but that he almost got away with it.

The final and perhaps greatest difference between murder in fiction and in life is pain. In fiction, the suffering, not just of the victim but of those left behind (whose pain is often worse because it lasts so long), is largely left out. In life it is achingly, shockingly apparent. Paul Wilkinson has created enormous pain in many people—he has shattered lives that can never be made whole again. To what he has done by killing Kylie Labouchardiere he has added the cruelty of not saying where he buried her.

This book is dedicated to Wilkinson's other victims: to Kylie's grandmother Louisa; her parents, John and Carol; her sister, Leanne, and brother, Michael; and her ex-husband, Sean. It is also dedicated to those members of the police force, especially Glenn Smith and Rebekkah Craig, who through their persistence brought Paul Wilkinson to justice.

MISSING

John Edwards' nightmare began when his phone rang at mid-day on Saturday 8 May 2004, and it has continued to this day. When he thinks about his life now, he divides it into the time before that and the time after.

John had three children, Leanne, Michael and Kylie, all in their twenties. They lived on the Central Coast near their mother, Carol, from whom he was long separated. It was Michael on the phone, ringing to say they hadn't seen Kylie since she'd gone away over a week earlier to stay with friends for a few days.

This was a worry, but not as much as it would have been with many people. Kylie, who was twenty-three, was something of a mystery to her family; for her to stay away without telling them was not necessarily cause for alarm. Until recently, she'd been married and living in Sydney, and they knew little of her life down there. A few weeks before, she'd walked out on her husband, Sean Labouchardiere, and also on the nursing course she'd just started, and come up to stay with her grandmother Louisa at Erina. She had no children and was not working. When she left ten days before, she hadn't said who she'd be staying with or for exactly how long. It was in keeping with her character that she'd change her plans and forget to call; her grandmother believed there was a new man in her life.

That was the positive view. But on the other hand, Kylie had been planning to go to Moree by train that morning with an uncle and aunt to attend a cousin's engagement party. The relatives had called Louisa to say Kylie had not turned up at Central: she'd missed the train, despite buying a ticket weeks ago. That was less like her, and this—along with the amount of time that had now passed without any communication—was why Michael had decided to call his father.

John considered what Michael told him. He felt uneasy, but he was not going to panic—he was not the panicking kind. John was fifty-one in 2004, an ex-soldier, still fit and tanned. Since leaving the army he had held responsible positions, run businesses and dealt with crises and people under pressure. He loved his daughter but was fully aware of her private nature, and her sometimes headstrong behaviour. Still, there was enough that was odd about the whole thing to make him uneasy, and he decided to drive up to Erina and talk to other members of the family to obtain more information. In the army John had worked at Victoria Barracks in a top-secret job in communications; he knew the value of intelligence.

The first part of the trip took him through the tangle

of roads in the city's west until he reached the F3, the big freeway connecting Sydney with the Central Coast. As he drove, he thought about the last time he'd seen Kylie, five weeks earlier. She'd come to visit him in Parramatta, where he worked with a company that helped people find jobs. He thought about her smile, because with Kylie the thing everyone noticed about her first was her smile—not just a grin but a big, toothy smile. She had inherited it from him.

When she was a child it had been a great smile, gaining her the nickname 'Smiley Kylie'. With her light-brown hair and chubby cheeks, that look in her brown eyes showing utter contentment, complete trust, she was everything you hoped a daughter might be. John remembers her as a happy child who would always hug people when she greeted them. But just before she turned five, John and Carol had separated, and before long Carol took up with a man named Robert McCann, a criminal and a man of violence, who had turned her life inside out. The children had gone to live with their grandmother but they'd continued to see their mother and McCann, and what he did to her. The effects had been particularly bad on Kylie.

When she came out of her childhood, the smile was still there but it was very different, showing a lot of strain. If you knew the story of her life, you might say she'd been wounded and had not recovered. She was just above average height and slender, with an open, bright face and hair, dyed blonde now, usually at shoulder length. She had a lively personality, although sometimes she could be moody.

John loved her more than ever and he hated what had happened because of the divorce and her mother's decade of abuse by McCann. You could see from Kylie's smile that she desperately wanted to be happy, but things had occurred that made her doubt whether anything good in her life would last. For a while there, in the early days of her marriage to Sean, the family had thought she might have broken through into a new life. But it had all gone bad, although they didn't know why. It was as though the past had reached out and pulled Kylie back.

When they'd met, Kylie told him she was leaving Sean. John had been surprised. On Christmas Eve the couple had invited the family to their townhouse at Sylvania for a meal, and as far as John could see, everything had been fine. And now this. He wondered if their separation had anything to do with their failure to have a baby. This mattered a lot to Kylie: she'd actually made a nursery in the spare room not long after the wedding, even stocking it with nappies and baby lotions. But they hadn't been married much more than a year: it seemed early to cut and run. Maybe something else had happened, but Kylie hadn't offered any more information.

About halfway through John's trip to the Coast, there occurred the first of what were to be several coincidences in the story of the last weeks of Kylie's life. Not long after the Calga Interchange, the broad freeway dips and sweeps across the Mooney Mooney Bridge, reputedly the tallest in the southern hemisphere. Years later, it would turn out to be linked to Kylie's disappearance. It's even possible John drove over his daughter's grave, seventy-five metres below, on his way north that day, although that grave has never been found.

But all that lay ahead. For now he just concentrated on the road, worked his way up to the Gosford exit and turned off onto the long highway that runs down to the Coast. He intended to talk to the family and search Kylie's room, try to find out where she was. He was going to use all his skills to find her and bring her back, make sure she had another chance. Make some sort of recompense for leaving her all those years before, when he'd walked away from Carol. Everyone deserved another chance, but Kylie deserved one more than most.

KYLIE

In the photos of John and Carol Edwards' wedding in Sydney in 1973, John looks happy, with a huge smile pushing his narrow cheeks into long creases. Carol, a short, solid woman, has her thick, dark hair rolled back above her forehead, and her fluffy white dress covers every inch of skin except her face and hands. She seems happy too, although there's a hint of wariness in other photos from around this period, which was to become more evident with time.

Before long, they had three children: Leanne in 1975, Michael in 1977, and Kylie Maree Edwards, born 16 September 1980. Carol became pregnant with Kylie by accident, and the couple's relationship deteriorated as the pregnancy progressed. Carol was a fragile woman who sometimes found the challenges of motherhood overwhelming. John was away a lot on military exercises, and she spent much time at the home of her parents, Louisa and Harry Windeyer, at Villawood in Sydney's west so they could help with the other children.

Kylie was a demanding baby. She rarely slept and she cried constantly, refusing to be with anyone but her mother. John was posted to New Guinea for three months, and Carol recalls being like a zombie. She moved back to the home of her parents, who grew close to the children; Harry called Kylie his sweet pea.

Soon after John returned to Australia, he was posted to Watsonia in Melbourne. The family went with him but Carol found it tough, having no family support and little time to make new friends. Life is often hard for army wives, and having three young children made it worse. Kylie was frequently very ill with tonsillitis, almost dying several times due to breathing difficulties. Louisa would fly down from Sydney to help Carol cope. John continued to be away from home frequently on army matters, and in April 1985 he announced he was leaving Carol. She packed her bags and took the children back to her parents' place.

Once settled in, she began to go out to a local club, the Chester Hill RSL, and made some friends. This was a new experience for her: she'd never smoked or drunk alcohol before, and since getting married at nineteen and having children, she'd almost never had the time to socialise. Now, at the age of thirty and with her parents available for baby-sitting, she was determined to make up for that.

But Carol was hurt and vulnerable, and had little experience of men. Within a few weeks she met Robert McCann and found herself attracted to him, even though he was ten years her junior. McCann wanted someone he could dominate, and Carol was perfect. After all the years of doing the right thing while bringing up the children, often feeling lonely, her self-esteem was low. Only a few months after separating from John, she left her parents and went to live with McCann, taking the children with her.

Before long he was hitting her. An officer from the Department of Community Services (DoCS) found out and said the department would remove her children if she stayed with him, because of the danger he posed to them. Carol felt she was being forced to choose between her children and the man she loved. She felt she'd been pushed around all her life, and now, when she'd finally found a chance of happiness, someone wanted to take it away from her. So she abandoned her children. In early 1986, Michael, Leanne and Kylie—aged eleven, nine and six—went to live with their grandparents in Villawood.

Carol says the decision to leave her children was a traumatic one, which she now deeply regrets; today she finds it hard to understand what she was going through at that time. One thing she does know is that DoCS' concerns were justified: years later, Kylie told her that McCann had already assaulted her twice by this time, once holding her out an upstairs window by her ankles and threatening to drop her, and once throwing her down a flight of stairs. At the time these attacks happened, Kylie was just four or five years old.

Losing her mother in this way, and later realising more fully how Carol had chosen her lover over her children, must have been deeply traumatic for Kylie, in ways most of us can only imagine. Leanne believes Kylie was probably more affected by it than she and Michael were, but has no idea to what extent. She doesn't know if anyone ever sat down with Kylie at the time and explained what was happening and why their mother had left. But the effects were deep and permanent: Kylie was a victim of life long before she became a victim of Paul Wilkinson.

Louisa brought the children up for the next decade. She performed the job almost single-handedly, because Harry died the following year. John had access to his children every second weekend. When Kylie started in kindergarten at Villawood East Primary School, she became hysterical every day when Leanne—who was an older pupil at the school—left her at 9.00 a.m. This went on for weeks, until the teachers prevented Leanne from waiting with her outside the classroom. After that, Kylie seems to have calmed down and enjoyed primary school. She grew closer to her grandmother, who provided an emotional and physical refuge from which the child was able to observe her mother's tortured second marriage.

A question raised years later by people familiar with Kylie's disappearance is why she would have entered an abusive relationship with a man like Paul Wilkinson. One possible reason is that as she grew up, her main experience of a relationship between a man and a woman was her mother's with Robert McCann. It lasted ten years, and Kylie visited her mother often, encountering McCann and seeing what he was doing to her. Maybe this conditioned the expectations she came to have of adult relationships. McCann was, after all, the man her mother loved—indeed, he was the man for whom she had abandoned Kylie and her other children.

McCann's father had been in the air force, so the family

moved around a lot in his youth. When he was fifteen his parents separated, and the next year he was convicted of multiple crimes—mainly stealing cars—and sent to Mount Penang Juvenile Detention Centre. He was a violent youth: one of his thefts had involved force, and in the year he met Carol he was charged with attacking another woman.

Carol and McCann married in March 1987. They both had jobs, she with the NRMA and he as a station assistant with the railways. She found him completely dominating. If a night went badly on the poker machines, he'd lock her out of the house. He took most of the money she earned and used it for drinking and gambling, and he insisted on seeing her financial records to make sure she was handing over everything. The couple spent their nights and weekends at clubs, drinking and playing the machines, except for the times he would head off into the darkness to do a bit of 'midnight shopping'. He would steal cars and buy wrecks of the same models, swapping the plates and chassis numbers before selling them on.

In 1988 McCann stopped working for the railways and Carol and he were evicted from their house in Villawood. He started committing more crime, culminating in an ambitious attempt to rob the cash box on a train. In January 1989, he and a partner, who was dressed in a guard's uniform, turned up on Platform 24 at Central Railway Station. Somehow the partner was able to take the place of a rostered guard on the service that collected the takings from railway stations, and he smuggled McCann on board.

Train 60A travelled to Bondi and down through the Shire to Waterfall, then back towards the city. Staff at each station put bags of cash in the locked steel box, and between stations McCann used tools he had brought with him to try to unbolt it from the floor. The getaway car was parked at Tempe, but when the train arrived there the box was still attached, so they went on, eventually throwing it off near Erskineville Station and jumping after it. The partner kept watch on the box, which was later found to contain $53,247.41, while McCann raced off to collect the car.

But they were caught, and in July McCann pleaded guilty to this and other offences; he was sentenced to seven years' jail, with a non-parole period of three years. It would have been longer except that McCann had given information to the police.

The next three years provided Carol with a respite, but when McCann got out of jail she took him back and the cycle of violence recommenced. Kylie—who hated the man and couldn't understand why her mother stayed with him—was now eleven.

Fortunately for the children, Louisa continued to provide an emotional centre for their lives. She later described Kylie as a private child who didn't like being told what to do and was snappy at times. She was a bit of a wanderer and could be unsettled, and liked doing things on her own. Outwardly she was an average sort of girl, not doing too well academically but enjoying sport, for a while playing with the Birrong Sports Netball Club. She was a happy-go-lucky kid in a casual world, wearing brightly coloured T-shirts tucked into loose shorts, usually with thongs. Her light-brown hair was cut just above her shoulders.

A change occurred at the end of primary school. Kylie

wanted to go on to Bass Hill High School, like all her friends, but Louisa insisted she go to Chester Hill High School because that's where Leanne and Michael were. (Leanne had started out at Bass Hill but switched because it was too rough.) At Chester Hill, Kylie became a rebel. When Leanne was sixteen she moved into a spare room in Louisa's garage and her friends would come over, some of them boys with cars. Over the next few years, Kylie was always trying to go out with the older kids. She showed off and sought their attention, but she didn't seem to have too many friends of her own.

Carol says that Kylie went off the rails in high school. She started skipping classes and Louisa was unable to control her. Often she would stay out until midnight. When she was thirteen or fourteen, she began to sleep over at the house of a boyfriend, Troy Myers, at Regents Park. For several years she lived there or at Louisa's, depending on the state of her relationship with Troy. His mother, Maxine Cahill, became a good friend, and Kylie called her 'Mum'.

Cahill doesn't remember a lot about Kylie at that age. She does recall that she knew how to have fun. They would all go driving together with music blaring out, and Kylie could be cheeky. She might call out to a man walking his dog, 'It's not nice to take your wife for a walk!' She was popular with boys but didn't have a lot of boyfriends. Later in her adolescence, she was interested in a policeman from Bass Hill but it didn't go anywhere. She didn't drink a lot or smoke, and had stopped playing much sport, although for a while she was a cheergirl for a rugby league team.

Kylie, says Cahill, 'loved to laugh and was very trusting.

She trusted too much, believed everything people would say.' It was an observation others would make in the years to come.

It was an uncertain adolescence and sometimes a violent one. One day in 1996, Kylie was umpiring a game of hockey at the Sefton Roller Rink when she was attacked by a boy who'd recently broken up with her best friend. The boy was under the impression Kylie had been spreading gossip about their break-up, and he struck her with his hockey stick. She fell to the ground but managed to get up and off the rink, where she sat down and took her skates off. She began to have trouble breathing so she walked over to the first-aid post and collapsed, unconscious. An ambulance took her to Auburn Hospital. The assault left her with sore ribs, blurred vision in her left eye and a numbness on the left side of her face. This developed into Bell's palsy, which caused that side of her face to droop for about a week.

Meanwhile, Carol's marriage with McCann continued and the violence got worse. He'd hold a knife to her throat and say, 'Ring your mother and say goodbye to her.' Carol says she was too scared to leave because McCann said that if she did, he would hurt her children. The injuries she suffered were extensive and serious, yet he got away with hurting her for a long time.

Years later, after her marriage broke up, Carol would give evidence against McCann in court after he was charged with assaulting her. A few details from the hearing give a sense of what she'd gone through. The transcript shows that, at first, the magistrate at Sutherland Local Court had difficulty grasping just how many assaults there were and how far back they stretched.

BENCH: Well, wait a minute, what are we talking about now? . . . I'll have to start again . . . 30 July 1988 [assault on Carol], that's the first assault occasioning [actual bodily harm]. The second assault occasioning matter that I have is between 1 January 1988 and 31 December 1988 at Fairfield, assault . . .

CRAWFORD-FISH [McCann's lawyer]: Yes, your worship, that's correct.

BENCH: The next matter I have is between 1 March 1991 and 31 March 1992 assault, common assault on Carol Anne McCann?

CRAWFORD-FISH: That's correct.

BENCH: The next matter I have is 26 November 1996 at Narellan, assault occasioning actual bodily harm on a person?

CRAWFORD-FISH: That's correct.

BENCH: And then malicious wounding between 15 October 1997 and 16 October at Chester Hill?

CRAWFORD-FISH: That's correct, your worship.

Behind this incomplete list lay the long and violent history of Carol's second marriage, part of the background to Kylie's childhood and adolescence. In his sentencing, the magistrate said McCann's offences 'fall into the most serious category as far as the assault occasioning [bodily harm] matters are concerned in terms of the extreme violence that was used . . . They not only involve acts of violence but they involve acts of violence which resulted in substantial injuries on some occasions and the implements used to inflict those injuries include . . . tennis rackets, cricket bats and there was even a threat with a knife.' He sentenced McCann, who had pleaded guilty at the last minute, to nine months' periodic detention.

Despite the assaults listed above, and all the others, Carol continued to live with McCann through the second half of the 1990s. After every attack she told herself, 'I've got over this hurdle,' and hoped things would get better. This is quite common with domestic violence, where victims often return to their abusers a number of times before leaving for good. Things didn't get better for Carol, whom McCann continued to hit and abuse and belittle and isolate.

She decided to withhold a small amount of her wages from him and put it in a bank account. One night he went through her bag and found the bank book. This started a massive argument, and he bashed her and grabbed a knife and stabbed her. Then he threw her out of the house and onto a marble walkway and slammed the door. There was blood everywhere and Carol had several broken ribs. Somehow she managed to get up and started to walk towards her mother's place, but before long she collapsed on the footpath. There she was found at 2.00 a.m. by Kylie, who had been out and was walking home. She helped Carol to Louisa's and called a doctor. He wanted her to have McCann charged with assault but she refused. Carol says Kylie went back to her place with an iron bar but McCann refused to open the door. Kylie sought psychiatric help after this incident: she wanted to kill both her stepfather and herself.

Carol was taken up to her sister Joy's place at Green Point north of Sydney, a region known as the Central Coast or, to locals, simply as the Coast. But once she'd recovered, she went back to McCann. He still had total control over her and kept her as isolated as possible from other people, always wanting to know where she was, checking the grocery dockets to see how much she'd spent. The violence became even more frequent. Finally, on 30 July 1998, it came to a head. They were at the club in the evening and he asked her for more money to put through the machines. She told him he couldn't have any and left the club by herself. He followed her out in a fury and attacked her on the street, bashing and kicking.

Kylie actually witnessed some of this assault. She was driving past in a friend's car and saw McCann hit Carol in the face. 'That was my mother,' Kylie said to the driver.

'Are you sure?'

'I think I know my own mother! Turn around and go to the police station!'

When they arrived, Kylie ran inside and said, 'My mum is being bashed on the corner.' Two police raced to the scene and spoke with the couple. When Kylie later saw Carol, she had a lot of blood on her face and clothes, and cuts to her nose and lip, a swollen right eye and cheek, and grazes and abrasions on her left elbow and her hands.

Carol was taken to Bankstown Hospital, where she spent three weeks and had part of her face rebuilt. She describes this as a turning point in her life. An apprehended violence order was taken out on McCann, and after Carol was released from hospital she spent three months in a refuge, away from Sydney so he couldn't find her. She decided to move to the Coast, where her mother now lived at Erina. The night of the attack was the last time she saw McCann, apart from when she went to court to give evidence against him a few years later.

Kylie had one more encounter with her stepfather. Her relationship with Troy Myers had ended, and when she was eighteen she began going out with Dean Lucan, a young bartender at the Regents Park Bowling Club. He was a quiet man, a champion at lawn bowls, and Kylie started to play too. They lived together in a flat in Auburn and things seemed to be going well. The family say Dean was a calm young man and had a calming effect on Kylie while they were together.

One Friday night in 1999, they were in the club with two other people after closing time, having a drink while Dean counted the night's takings. Suddenly a masked man wielding a pistol came in and pointed the gun at Kylie's head. He yelled at Dean, 'If you know what's good for you, you'll pack the money in the bag, or she's going to get it!'

Dean gave the man the money and he left. Kylie was sure it was Robert McCann. She told the police of her suspicions, but there was insufficient evidence and he was never charged with the robbery. Carol says that after this Kylie became depressed, had counselling and left Dean. She went to live for a while with Louisa.

Robert McCann continued to attack women and, like many abusers, to deny responsibility for his actions. In 2002 he was convicted of bashing and raping his flatmate, an Asian student. He proclaimed his innocence, and at his sentencing, when his record of violence during his marriage came up, he said, 'I never deliberately set out to hurt or harm my wife.' He accused Carol of behaving in a manner 'that triggered off my behaviour'. He was sentenced to a jail term of at least four years and nine months.

★

After leaving Dean, Kylie started a relationship with a man named Ben in Victoria. Carol thinks she might have met him on the internet. Ben came up to meet the family, and it turned out he was from a big, religious family. Without warning, Kylie packed her bags and moved to Melbourne, where by December 2000 she'd got a flat by herself at Moonee Ponds and a job at Coles. She also did some work as a nurse's assistant: she'd always been interested in helping people professionally and had done some volunteer work as an ambulance officer.

Ben lived with his family not far from Kylie's new home. Leanne thinks he was a Catholic and that Kylie might have become a Catholic for a while. Carol thought they were lovely people, but she didn't think that Ben, who was interested in computers, was Kylie's sort. One night Kylie went to a restaurant with Ben's family and met Sean Labouchardiere. He was thirty years old, ten years older than her, a handsome man with blond hair, and had been in the navy for six years. Based in Sydney, he'd come to Melbourne to sit an examination for the police force, thinking he might like a change.

They got talking and Sean gave Kylie a lift home from the restaurant, and the next day after he did the police exam he found her waiting for him. That night they watched some videos at her place. Sean returned to Sydney and Kylie started sending him five to ten text messages a day. She said her relationship was in trouble and asked Sean if he'd go out with her if she broke up with Ben. Sean would later learn that this was one of Kylie's characteristics: she was great one for change but liked to plan her changes in advance. He agreed with her suggestion.

He transferred to Melbourne and they began to see each other. She was loud, sometimes stroppy, while he was quiet. He liked the fact she was an easy-going woman with no airs and graces. She dressed in jeans or tracksuit pants, T-shirt or casual jacket, and enjoyed the classic Aussie bands from when she was growing up, Cold Chisel and INXS. She was a very organised person: she kept a diary and was always thinking about what she was going to do. He visited her at work at a nursing home and saw how well she got on with the patients.

Their relationship was hugely important to Kylie because there were few people in her life. At first she had little to say about her family, and Sean gained the impression she was running away from some problem. She would ring her grandmother Louisa every week, but apart from that there was almost no contact. She had no friends in Melbourne and the couple spent most of their free time with Sean's family.

After a while, Kylie told him some of her background, how she'd been brought up by Louisa and Maxine Cahill, the hold-up and the counselling she'd had afterwards, and a policeman she'd gone out with for a short time until something happened at work; one night he had pulled out his gun and threatened her. Another boyfriend, she said, had been violent towards her. She appeared to have got over these experiences and was generally bright and bubbly, which Sean liked. At times, though, there was something a little forced in her cheerfulness, and occasionally she'd become angry for no apparent reason. But these were only minor things.

By April 2001 they had left Melbourne and were living together in a flat at Erina. Kylie's relations with her family picked up, and now Sean and she spent time with Louisa,

Carol, Leanne and her two young daughters, and Michael. In Melbourne Kylie had been concerned about what he would think of her family. His own was intact and pretty typical, while hers, obviously, was not. But at Erina they got on well enough: each side made an effort, and Sean soon felt accepted.

He discovered Kylie didn't have any friends on the Coast, or even in Sydney. She told him everyone she'd been to school with was either dead or in prison. This solitariness was unusual but had its benefits for a sailor's wife: Kylie was independent and happy to fit in with Sean's postings around the country, at least in those early days. Not all partners were so flexible.

Kylie got a job at a nursing home in North Sydney, and Sean was stationed at HMAS *Penguin*, conveniently nearby in Mosman. She would turn up at the base during the day and sometimes in the evening, expecting to be able to hang out with him. This was unusual and he had to explain that she couldn't come to his work all the time because he was getting in trouble. She had difficulty understanding this and they argued.

As Sean got to know Kylie better, he found she had a frustrated desire to help people. Whenever she met anyone of any age who was in some sort of strife, she'd do her best to assist them, sometimes even taking on too much. At work she would ring patients once their treatment was finished to see how they were. Once she got to know Sean's family, she took an interest and would call them on their birthdays. At Erina she would sometimes look after Leanne's girls and buy them presents. Sean found all this very appealing. She began to talk about studying to become a registered nurse. She hadn't done it before because she'd thought she wouldn't be able to handle the demands of university, but the more she worked in nursing homes, the more confident she became. She was fascinated by people in uniform, and gradually her desire to become a nurse grew.

As they became closer, Kylie told Sean more about her unstable upbringing, which included plenty of experience of violence and other effects of alcoholism. She still seemed to resent her mother for what she had done, although she didn't talk about it much. As he came to love her she seemed happier, and he wanted to make her contented, to give her a settled home. They decided to get married, and to announce this at Kylie's twenty-first birthday party in September 2001.

Kylie wore a dark-blue satin dress for the event; her hair was dyed a light blonde and elaborately teased into curls. She looked happy but also a little startled, as though nervous at being the centre of attention. Compared with his wedding photo of some twenty-eight years earlier, John hadn't changed much, at least outwardly. The warmth was still in his eyes, but if you looked carefully, the confidence of his earlier years was diminished. He'd remarried and just come through a bad divorce, the emotional effects putting him into South Pacific Private Hospital for a while at the beginning of the year. But he was getting over it now, and for the next six years would work part-time as a volunteer in the hospital, helping other people deal with their problems. It was a period of personal growth for him: as he grew older, he mellowed from the disciplinarian he had once been and developed a modest sense of humour.

In the photos from the twenty-first party, Carol is bigger

than she'd been at her wedding and a certain unhappy tenseness is set in her expression. Michael once observed that Kylie was the sibling closest to their mother, and you can see it in their eyes, a wariness that seems out of place on such an occasion. Possibly it was part of their nature but also a reaction to life as both mother and daughter had experienced it.

The wedding was not to be held for more than a year, but Kylie took on the job of organising it and began immediately. The job brought her out of herself, gave her a goal and, even more, almost a new identity as a future wife with the right to assert herself, at least with regard to the marriage plans. The planning was meticulous, with Kylie insisting everything be done exactly as she wanted. She wasn't good at negotiating disagreement: at one point she went right over the top and fell out with Sean's sisters. They had been going to be bridesmaids but couldn't live up to Kylie's demands.

In August Kylie was quite stressed by all the planning, so Sean and she took a holiday in Tasmania. Sean did all the driving, as he usually did when they were together, and they enjoyed the restaurants in Hobart and the bushwalking at Cradle Mountain. It was an early honeymoon, and marked the beginning of the best period of their relationship.

In October 2002 Sean was posted back to Melbourne, and the wedding took place at St David's Anglican Church in East Doncaster in January 2003. Kylie wore a simple white dress with a multi-coloured bouquet. Carol had chosen a red suit for the occasion, while Leanne, the matron of honour, wore yellow. Michael was in formal black and Sean, his blond hair cut short, was grinning with delight.

John and Carol each looked at the young couple and

thought about the choices they'd made in their own relation-ships, and the effects those choices had had on their daughter. They hoped that she had found the stability and happiness she craved and deserved, and which they wanted her so very much to have. Sean was good for Kylie: she seemed to have grown up a lot in the past year.

Leanne also believed that Kylie's life had turned around. The sisters had never been close. Apart from the five-year gap in ages, there was a big difference in their characters, with Leanne calm and mistrustful of the love of drama Kylie had inherited from their mother. Kylie was an attention-seeker and was drawn towards danger, qualities that frankly scared Leanne. She'd seen her sister grow into a woman who was always either hyper-cheerful or moody, and who resented any attempt at a serious conversation as an intrusion into her private world.

But lately she'd changed. Leanne looked forward to a future when Kylie and Sean would buy a house and have children, a future when the sisters would be able to talk prop-erly and grow close, for the first time in their often difficult and troubled lives. Leanne believed the gap between Kylie and herself—in maturity and circumstances—was shrinking: Kylie was finally catching up.

THE FATHER

As John headed down the Central Coast Highway in May 2004, he recalled the details of his recent encounter with Kylie, when she'd visited him at work in Parramatta. After announcing her separation from Sean, she said she was staying with Louisa at Erina, where an agent was holding a flat for her. If John could give her $500 she could move in the next day. He pressed her for more information and she admitted she needed $1500 in total; she was hoping to get the rest from her grandmother. John said he'd give her the full amount and offered to write a cheque. Kylie said she needed it that day, so after she left he used the internet to transfer the money into her account. He rang her that night on her mobile and confirmed she'd received it.

The next day he'd called to see how things were going. This time he rang the landline and talked with Louisa, who told him Kylie wasn't staying there at all. He figured he'd been caught up in one of Kylie's dramas—maybe she did need the money for a flat, despite the lie about where she was living, or maybe it was for something else. He decided not to pursue the matter for the moment; Kylie could tell him what was really going on in her own good time.

Now he wondered some more about the money. According to what Michael had told him on the phone, Kylie had not come to live with Louisa until a few weeks after the meeting at Parramatta, and she hadn't taken out a lease on a flat. The money must have been for something else. Maybe she was involved in something dangerous, although he had no idea what. Maybe she was in hiding. Disturbing thoughts ran through his mind as he reached Gosford, the region's biggest town.

The Central Coast was once a string of holiday and retirement beaches connected to Sydney by a road so tortuous that commuting was out of the question. But with the building of the freeway, daily travel to the city became feasible, and in the 1980s the Coast began to grow into what it is today: a region of some 300,000 people sprawled among attractive beaches, waterways and bushland. Many of the new residents came from Sydney's western suburbs, prompted to move by changes brought about by high levels of immigration and poor government. Roads became clogged, public transport was overburdened and house prices shot up and became unaffordable for many young couples. Tens of thousands moved up to the Coast in search of a more relaxed environment in which to retire or bring up children.

Erina is a suburb of Gosford. John reached Louisa's flat at 1.30 p.m., when he had the first of what would be many conversations with her and the rest of the family. She described how at 6.15 p.m. on Wednesday 28 April, Kylie had left the flat and walked across the road to the bus stop, where she took the service to Gosford Railway Station. She was hauling two bags, had her hair tied back in a ponytail, and was wearing a red and green Rabbitohs zip-up jacket, jeans and white sneakers. A few hours later, she'd called Louisa to say she'd arrived at Central Railway Station in Sydney. That was the last time anyone in the family had heard from her.

John asked about Kylie's behaviour over the past few weeks. The more he learned, the more confusing the story became: Kylie's recent life had been even more eventful than he'd realised. For a start, apparently she'd been raped by a friend of Sean's two months earlier. John was shocked by this news, which set his thoughts off in new directions. He wondered if the rapist might have had anything to do with her disappearance, but it seemed unlikely: he lived interstate.

There were more surprises, and also plenty of confusion. While some members of the family believed Kylie was going to visit friends, she'd told others she'd decided to become a police officer and was off to the Police Academy at Goulburn to commence her training. But in confidence she'd told Louisa something else entirely: she was pregnant. The father wasn't Sean. Nor was it the alleged rapist, who had worn a condom. It says something about Kylie's character, and her relationship with her family, that she'd been able to parcel out all these dramatic secrets, which only now were being fully shared and compared.

When Kylie hadn't come home after a week, Louisa thought she might be spending time with the man who'd got her pregnant—whoever that might be. The family speculated on this now, and the others told John of changes they'd noticed in Kylie when she had moved to Louisa's a few weeks earlier. She swore a lot, which was new, and was more aggressive. She'd also taken up smoking—although that had stopped abruptly about a fortnight ago, perhaps when she'd discovered she was pregnant. There was also a new enthusiasm for the South Sydney rugby league team, which was unusual because Kylie had no connection they were aware of with Redfern, Souths' heartland, and had not even followed league in recent years.

Another major puzzle was that the day after Kylie left, a removalist firm had rung Louisa. They said Kylie had sent her furniture (which had been in storage since her split with Sean) to the inland city of Dubbo, and had arranged to meet them there that day but hadn't turned up. This was strange, although it might possibly fit in with one of Kylie's stories: maybe she was planning to move to Dubbo with her child's father, and had sent her furniture ahead.

The family, as they now explained to John, had been concerned enough to do some investigating before they contacted him. Leanne had rung Sutherland Hospital, where Kylie had been working until recently as a nursing assistant, and tried without success to find out who her friends were. Leanne wanted to talk with them to ask if they were the people Kylie had gone to Sydney to visit. But the only response was speculation Kylie might be in a woman's refuge somewhere. Some months earlier, she'd told colleagues she was having marriage problems.

John asked the others more about this, wondering if Sean

might have anything to do with Kylie's disappearance. It didn't seem likely: despite the sudden collapse of the marriage, there'd been no hint of violence from Sean, who was a mild-mannered sort of bloke. The family said they had no reason to think the two had met since Kylie left him.

Once Louisa had become seriously worried about the lack of contact from Kylie, she'd gone into her room and found two recent monthly phone accounts; she was surprised to see how big they were: $800 and $1300. They showed that Kylie had been in constant contact with one number in particular, and when Michael next came over, on 7 May, he'd called it.

'You have reached Paul Wilkinson,' said a recorded voice. 'Leave your name and message.'

No one in the family had ever heard the name Paul Wilkinson. Michael hung up without leaving a message. Fifteen minutes later his mobile received a text message: 'There was a missed call from your number, who are you.' Michael rang again and a man answered. 'Are you Paul Wilkinson?' Michael said. 'I'm Kylie's brother.'

'I didn't know she had a brother,' said the man.

'Have you seen her lately?'

'The last time I heard from her was the Monday before she left.'

'You're sure?' said Michael.

'Yeah.'

It was a noisy phone call: Michael could hear a woman's voice in the background, and a baby was making a lot of noise. Recalling Kylie's story about joining the police, he said to Wilkinson, 'Are you a copper?'

'Yeah. How did you know that?' Wilkinson suggested

Michael tell the local police at Gosford that Kylie was missing, and mention his name. 'If you hear from her, can you give me a call?' he said. And then, 'If you're around some time we could meet up. I work in Sydney.' The background noise increased and Wilkinson rang off, saying he would call Michael later.

When Wilkinson hadn't called back later that day, Leanne rang and asked if he'd heard from Kylie.

'No,' said Wilkinson, 'not since Monday. How did your brother know I was a cop?' He sounded concerned about this, which Leanne thought odd.

'I don't know,' she said. 'Where are you based?'

'Sydney. I can tell you something. I don't know whether you know or not . . . I am dealing with something to do with Kylie now. I'm at Miranda Police Station because she filed a rape charge, and it's a hoax—she's filed a false statement.'

Leanne said, 'How did you get this information? How did they [the police] find out about this rape charge? Have they found it out by investigation or word from her?'

'From her.'

Leanne was confused and concerned. 'What do you think will happen to her for putting in a false statement?'

'It's pretty serious,' said Wilkinson, 'but it's up to the detectives dealing with the case.'

'Are you at work now?'

'No, I'm based at Marrickville, but I'm not working at the moment as I've been a bad boy.' As he said this, Wilkinson giggled. This was the second thing about him that struck Leanne as unusual.

'Okay,' she said, 'we won't go there. Where do you fit in with Kylie? How do you know her?'

Wilkinson said they'd met in 1999, when she'd been working at the Rachel Foster Hospital in Redfern. He'd helped her out when she'd had trouble with Aboriginal kids trying to rob her as she walked to work from the railway station; she had come into Redfern Police Station for help. In 2003 they'd come across each other again by accident at Miranda Fair, the enormous shopping mall that services the suburbs of the Sutherland Shire in Sydney's south. They'd kept in touch.

Leanne said, 'We're all a bit concerned about Kylie . . . She hasn't made contact with the family in a week and a half. We'd really appreciate it if you could tell us anything.'

'If it was my sister,' said Wilkinson, 'I'd go straight down to the local police station and report her missing. Where is your local station?'

'Gosford.'

'Go down there and tell them what you know. The detectives need something to do up there—and can I ask you a favour? Can you give them my name and number . . . don't forget to give them my name and number.'

'I won't.'

'I know how you feel,' said Wilkinson. 'My brother went missing for three months—it's hard. Just go straight down there and report it, and give them my name and number. You can call me any time.'

'Thanks for your time,' said Leanne, and hung up. She was in a daze and wondered what it all meant. Later, she would wonder even more about Wilkinson's insistence that the family mention his name to the police at Gosford. It was as though he was trying to insert himself into the investigation.

Half an hour after Leanne's call, Wilkinson called Michael and said he'd just come out of Miranda Police Station. 'Kylie's sent me a text,' he said. 'It said the rape allegation is false. Kylie has been having an affair with Gary [the name used in this book for the man she alleged raped her], and she's gone [interstate] to be with him.' He added, 'Make sure you report it to the police, and give them my number.'

The family were of course terrifically encouraged by this phone call from a man they believed to be a police officer, because it indicated Kylie was alive.

John learned about other inquiries the family had made. Carol, wondering about the possibility of a link between Wilkinson and Dubbo, due to the call from the removalists, had checked with directory assistance and found the number of a woman named Wilkinson there. She rang, but the woman said she did not know a Paul Wilkinson. Michael had rung the removalists to see if Kylie had turned up; she hadn't. Her possessions had been stored at Ark Self Storage and she owed them $200 on the deposit.

Once he'd heard all these stories, John decided to search Kylie's room thoroughly. He found her diaries and other documents, and two cards in the drawer of the bedside table. The first was for Louisa:

Dear Grandma, Thank you! Grandma you are one in a million. I am very lucky to have such a loving caring grandma as you. Thank you for supporting me over the weeks I really appreciated it. I love you and know that this will always be my home. Love Kylie XXX

The second was for Leanne. Kylie had written:

Dear Leanne, Thank you!!! It really did mean a lot to me borrowing your car. Thank you for giving me the freedom to be able to use it whenever. You are a great sister and mean a lot to me. Thank you once again. Love always, Kylie

This supported the possibility Kylie had planned to move to Dubbo, but there were too many problems with what had happened next. Why hadn't she given the cards to Louisa and Leanne before she went? Why hadn't she been in touch? Why had she sent her furniture to Dubbo and then failed to go there? And where did the pregnancy, and the rape story, and Paul Wilkinson fit in?

John thought about everything he'd heard that afternoon and made a decision. At 4.00 p.m., he and Michael drove to Gosford Police Station in Mann Street. It's a sand-coloured four-storey building, and John was to see far too much of it in the years ahead. They parked outside and went into the front area, where they told the officer behind the counter they wanted to report Kylie as a missing person.

FIRE

Some 10,000 people are reported missing each year in the state of New South Wales, and in many cases their relatives assure police their absence is not typical of their normal behaviour. Despite this, nearly all the missing soon reappear, and it turns out their absence was completely voluntary. And even when they don't come back and an investigation occurs, the missing person is usually found. Often it emerges that they went off deliberately, not wanting their families to know where they were. Because of this pattern, and because the cost of investigating all those disappearances immediately and fully would be enormous, the police usually don't do much at first, at least where an adult is concerned.

These were some of the considerations on the mind of the officer who spoke with John and Michael that afternoon. Kylie's disappearance was entered on COPS, the police operational database. Then the officer, after considering what had just been learned, decided that in this case there were enough suspicious aspects to warrant investigation, and rang up to the detectives' office on the second floor of the big concrete building. On duty that afternoon were senior constables Rebekkah Craig and Andrew Pace.

Craig would be the only officer involved in the investigation from start to finish. She was thirty-one and had grown up in Narrabri, joining the police force in 1998. After six months at the Police Academy in Goulburn, she'd been posted to Redfern, an area with a relatively big Aboriginal population. There are racial tensions in Redfern largely absent in other city police stations; these were to figure in the story of Kylie's disappearance.

Craig had married a fellow officer and transferred with him to Gosford in late 2003, thereby missing the Redfern Riots by a few months. These occurred on 14 February 2004, after a police car gave chase to a seventeen-year-old Aboriginal boy named Thomas Hickey—known as 'TJ'—who was riding a bicycle. There was an outstanding arrest warrant for Hickey, who in his attempts to escape lost control of his bicycle and was impaled on a metal fence and died. (There were conflicting accounts of his death. This is the authoritative one reached by the coronial inquest.) Aboriginal people from around Sydney gathered in Redfern and, claiming the police had killed TJ by ramming his bicycle and forcing him onto the metal spikes, rioted and injured many officers. From the safety of her new home on the Coast, Craig watched on television as her old general duties team, with Redfern Railway Station in flames, faced a mob of angry Aboriginal people, some hurling petrol bombs. She was glad she'd left.

It's not uncommon these days to see policewomen so small you wonder how they can carry their enormous equipment belts. Craig is not like this. She's an attractive woman with light-brown hair and a tan, and carries herself with a confidence backed by physical strength. At Redfern she'd been put on plainclothes duties in the detectives' office, not really wanting to leave uniform but finding after a while that she liked criminal investigative work. In 2004 she began the twelve-month detectives' course, a mix of work at Gosford (which came to include the investigation into Kylie's disappearance) and stints back at the academy.

One thing that struck her immediately when she sat down with John Edwards was the name Paul Wilkinson. Craig had actually worked with him when she was stationed at Redfern—Wilkinson had been there too, one of several Aboriginal Community Liaison Officers. An ACLO acts as a sort of buffer between police and the Aboriginal people they deal with. ACLOs must be at least part-Aboriginal—Wilkinson has an Aboriginal mother—but they are not police officers. (There are still relatively few Aboriginal cops in New South Wales.) In essence, their job is to explain the police point of view to Aboriginal people and vice versa, in situations of conflict or potential conflict. It's an important job but a difficult one, because each side suspects the ACLO's first loyalty lies with its opponent. Some ACLOs handle this tension better than others.

In Craig's experience, Wilkinson had been friendly and generally competent, and others who worked with him at Redfern say the same thing. But she'd never been quite sure about him because of one peculiarity. Whenever a police officer at Redfern arrested an Aboriginal person and brought them into the holding cells, the procedure was to do nothing more until an ACLO had a word with them, making sure they knew what was happening and were aware of their rights. Craig noticed that after Wilkinson talked with someone she'd arrested, they were often more hostile than when she brought them in. This surprised her—the ACLO's job was to achieve the opposite outcome—but it hadn't been a big enough deal for her to make anything of it. Wilkinson had moved from Redfern to Marrickville in July 2003, and—Craig was later to learn—had walked off the job there in February 2004 and was no longer working.

Now, in an interview room at Gosford, Craig looked at the phone bills John had just given her and saw that they showed thousands of calls and texts between Kylie and Wilkinson in recent months. Clearly there'd been some sort of relationship, and right away she had an uneasy feeling about Wilkinson's involvement. It wasn't something she could put into words but, like all good cops, she knew gut instincts can be important. She told John and Michael she'd look into Kylie's disappearance.

A few days later Craig called Wilkinson, and after they'd exchanged greetings she asked how he knew Kylie. He repeated the story he'd told Leanne Edwards, about first meeting Kylie at Redfern Police Station some years earlier and coming across her later at Miranda. He said they'd been friendly since then, although nothing more. Then he started to expand, saying Kylie had mentioned self-harm. He claimed she'd tried to hurt herself before and run off—he thought she'd been placed in psychiatric care against her will at one point—and said that recently she'd borrowed $500 to buy cannabis. He said that while Kylie had informed her family she was going to the Police Academy, she had actually been going to Sutherland Railway Station to meet an unknown person. This was presented in a rambling manner that Craig was to become familiar with.

For someone her family had never heard of until a few days ago, Wilkinson seemed to know a lot about Kylie. And he sounded nervous. Craig said, 'Obviously, we need to speak to you, Paul. Can you come in?' She was hoping he'd come up to Gosford: she knew she would be working Kylie's case along with an already busy schedule, and didn't want to spend a day going to and from the city to take a statement. But Wilkinson was hesitant, so she said, 'How about I come to Sydney?'

'No, no, no, don't come here,' he said. 'I'll come to you. I'm busy. I can't catch up with you this week.'

At that stage Craig wasn't sufficiently worried to push things, so they made an appointment for 1.00 p.m. the next Monday. There were plenty of other jobs to be getting on with.

On 10 May, she and Pace went to Louisa's house and searched Kylie's bedroom, from which they took a hairbrush and a toothbrush in case they needed a DNA profile for her. They read the cards addressed to Louisa and Leanne, which John had told them about. One thing they'd been wondering was whether Kylie might have committed suicide—this is always a consideration when someone goes missing for no apparent reason. Craig thought the cards, which had been written recently (because of the reference to Leanne lending

Kylie her car), suggested otherwise. They indicated that she had been intending to move out of Louisa's place and make a new start. (Presumably this move was not the train trip she'd made on 28 April: if it had been, Kylie would have given them the cards before she left.) Further evidence suggesting Kylie had not been suicidal included lay-by dockets from Big W and Target dating back only a week or two, and the opinion of her doctor, who'd seen her five times in the three months before she disappeared, that she had seemed happy enough.

The detectives talked to Louisa about Kylie's financial circumstances; they learned she was receiving Centrelink payments and had recently borrowed $700 from her grandmother. They spoke with other members of the family and encountered the same problem John had. Kylie had told different people significantly different stories about her life and her plans. This was fairly unusual in a missing person investigation, and it was a problem for the police. It meant they had to look at multiple theories for her disappearance and it raised the possibility that all her stories might be false: if Kylie had lied to one relative, why not to all of them?

Some of the things they found in her room were odd. There were cassettes of telephone conversations she'd recorded, and a transcript of a conversation she'd had in her home with Sean. Craig found this bizarre: it was as though Kylie had been conducting some sort of private investigation, although there was no hint as to why she would have done this.

Back at the office, the detectives commenced the standard checks. Craig's first request for Kylie's phone records was knocked back by a senior officer who did not consider the matter serious enough yet. She pursued other lines of inquiry, checking with the Austrac reporting system to confirm that Kylie had not made any recent financial transactions over $10,000. Pace obtained CCTV footage from the Erina Commonwealth Bank ATM at 11.00 a.m. on the day she went missing, plus footage of her from Erina Blockbuster Video the day before. The detectives called various financial institutions to find out about Kylie's bank accounts; they discovered that in recent months she'd maxed out her credit cards and borrowed almost $20,000 from various sources. They went back to the family but no one had any idea what had happened to this money. (Eventually they found the full amount of borrowings was closer to $24,000, all of which had disappeared.) On 11 May, Craig sent a statewide email to all NSW police, asking them to keep an eye out for Kylie.

Apart from Wilkinson, there were two other 'persons of interest', as police call possible suspects. These were Kylie's husband, Sean Labouchardiere, and his friend Gary, whom she alleged had raped her. Craig rang Sean, who confirmed that Kylie and he had separated. On the night she disappeared he'd been at home by himself. He said she had borrowed $3000 from him in March but had refused to say what it was for. As far as he knew, she did not have any mental-health issues. The detectives later took several statements from Sean and decided he'd had nothing to do with Kylie's disappearance.

Wilkinson had told Michael Edwards that Kylie had moved interstate to live with Gary, the man she claimed had raped her. Before talking with Gary, Craig needed to know more about the alleged rape. She obtained a copy of the statement

Kylie had made to Detective Sergeant Donna O'Mally at Cronulla Police Station on 9 March 2004.

Kylie recounted how Gary, whom she'd met with Sean before, had called them and said he was coming to Sydney on 19 February on a business trip, and the three of them should meet up. They agreed, but then Sean was 'crashposted'— ordered to sea at short notice—so Kylie went to see him by herself. It was 9.00 p.m. and she'd just finished her shift at Sutherland Hospital, having changed out of her uniform into a white padded bra and white G-string, a white Puma singlet top, navy blue track pants and joggers. When she reached the city she had called Gary at his hotel and asked if he wanted to come out and have coffee, but he suggested she come to his room. She got there and found him wearing a white T-shirt and beige shorts. They hugged briefly at the door and sat down and talked, and after a while Gary told her he and his wife hadn't had sex since Christmas. 'Why is that?' she'd said. 'Is everything all right between you guys?' He said it was, but she knew there was a problem.

Gary showed her some photos he'd taken with his digital camera and they went onto the balcony and looked at the view. Then they came inside and Gary opened the mini-bar and said he could take whatever he liked from it at his employer's expense. He lay down on the big bed and suggested Kylie lie down too. He said it a few times and after a while she lay down and they watched the television, which had been on all the time. At one point they talked about the recent Jewel concert, and Gary said, 'I've always liked blondes.'

'Oh, great,' joked Kylie, whose hair was blonde at the time, 'I'll have to dye my hair now.' They watched television some more, then Gary rolled over and started prodding her arm and ribs with a finger.

'What are you doing?' she said.

'I always fantasised about you,' he said, laughing.

'I'm married, Gary.'

He seemed angry, and got up and switched off the television. Then he turned off the room's light and went into the bathroom. When he came back into the room, which was dark, he got back onto the bed and came close to her, and she realised he'd taken his clothes off. He climbed on top of her and she put her hands up against his chest.

'Gary, stop what you're doing,' she said.

He repeated, 'I've always fantasised about you.' He started kissing her neck and she moved around, trying to avoid him, but he took no notice. He sat up and pulled down her track pants and then her G-string.

'Gary, no, stop,' she kept saying. 'What are you doing?'

Kylie told Donna O'Mally, in her sworn statement, that she hadn't yelled because she was scared he might hurt her if she made a noise. Then he got back on top of her again and raped her. He was wearing a condom. She felt powerless and scared but there was nothing she could do. He kissed her neck some more, and when it was over said, 'You're not to say a word about this to anyone.' He said it in a threatening tone and she feared for her life. When he got off her, he went into the bathroom and she stood up, pulled up her pants, grabbed her bag and went to walk out the door. Gary came out and switched the light on.

'Thanks for coming,' he said. 'I'll call you.'

Kylie told O'Mally that when she got home she was feeling

dirty and took off her clothes. She had a shower, soaping herself up three times and shampooing her hair. She got into her pyjamas and went to bed, where she slept poorly. At one point she got up and wrote an account of what had happened in her diary. The next morning she could smell Gary's aftershave on her clothes, so she washed them.

That was Kylie's statement. It raised a few questions, such as why Gary would rape the wife of a man he was so close to, why Kylie wouldn't have resisted more (Gary was neither strong nor fit), and how he thought he'd get away with it. There might well be answers to these questions, but at the moment they were puzzling. Turning from what Kylie had told O'Mally, Craig read what she'd written about the incident in her diary.

'Wrote out statement of what Gary did to me last night,' it began. 'Even though he had threatened me not to say anything. I wrote it down and kept it hidden in my drawer. I feel tired and scared as I didn't sleep that much last night. I was frightened that Gary was going to come back and do something to me. I wish that Sean was here. I wish that I could talk to him. Please Sean come home.'

But Sean was at sea on HMAS *Newcastle*. He came back on 25 February but Kylie didn't tell him she'd been raped until 3 March. This raised another question: why, if she was desperate for him to come back so she could talk to him, would she wait almost a week before saying anything? Again, there might be an answer to this question: victims of crime do not always act in a normal manner. But it was another puzzle.

One of the handwritten documents found in Kylie's room apparently recorded an exchange of text messages with Gary that had occurred in the days after the rape. Part of it went like this:

> Kylie: 'I cant handle this anymore I am going to tell Sean.'
>
> Gary: 'Tell him what.'
>
> Kylie: 'What happened.'
>
> Gary: 'What happened?'
>
> Kylie: 'What you did to me.'
>
> Gary: 'Sorry you have lost me in this I don't know what you are talking about.'
>
> Kylie: 'In Sydney.'
>
> Gary: 'Are you OK. Did I do something wrong.'
>
> Kylie: 'Yes everything you did was wrong and no I am not OK.'
>
> Gary: 'I will call U 2morrow is that OK.'
>
> Kylie: 'No dont call me I am telling Sean.'
>
> Gary: 'I cant figure out what you are on about but if you want an excuse to end your marriage which is what it sounds like then don't involve me and my family you are playing with peoples lives childrens lives!'

The same document contains what seems to be a transcript of the conversation when Kylie finally told Sean about the rape. She was sitting on the bed in their room and said she had to tell him something.

'What's wrong?' he said. 'Is it your job, uni, your family?'

Kylie burst into tears and told him Gary had raped her. Sean came over and sat down next to her on the bed and hugged her. He was upset and angry but also confused. It didn't sound like Gary at all. He rang Gary's mother, whom he knew very well, and told her what Kylie had said.

'It is not in his nature,' she said. 'It's very out of character. I'll speak to him about it.'

Later, Sean received a call from Gary, who said, 'What's going on? What did Kylie tell you?'

Sean said, 'You tell me what happened.'

'I've just spoken to Mum, and nothing happened in the hotel room, nothing at all. I've always thought of you as a brother. I can't believe you would think that I would do that to Kylie. I swear on my kid's grave that I would never do that to her.'

'Then why's Kylie said all these things?'

'I don't know.'

Sean said she planned to tell the police but Gary didn't seem concerned. 'It will be good,' he said. 'That'll clear my name. Then you can divorce her and we can get back to being friends.'

After Kylie went missing, Sean confirmed to police that she had told him about the alleged rape and a conversation such as that above did occur. He was still conflicted about what had happened, believing it highly unlikely that Gary would have done such a thing, but also believing that Kylie would not lie: the whole thing was a painful mystery.

According to Kylie's notes, on the same day as her conversation with Sean about the alleged rape she also told 'a guy called Paul Wilkinson'. She rang him at 9.00 p.m. and said, 'There's something I need to tell you.'

'What's wrong?'

'You remember when Gary was in Sydney?'

'Yes.'

'He sexually assaulted me.'

Wilkinson asked for details and told her she needed to go to the police station and make a formal statement. The next day she went to Miranda and reported the rape to Sergeant Di Stricker, and the day after that she had a phone conversation with Donna O'Mally. On 9 March, according to her diary, 'Went to Cronulla Police Station and made a statement about sexual assault. I found it very difficult and hard to re-live the past. I cried several times. Sgt. O'Mally took my statement. It went from 1400–1730 hrs. It was very traumatizing to go over the sexual assault.'

O'Mally was an experienced police officer, and certain aspects of Kylie's interview troubled her. Kylie appeared to have trouble recalling the sequence of events, and kept jumping back and forwards during the statement. Despite mentioning Paul Wilkinson, she seemed very keen to keep him out of the investigation. She said their relationship was purely professional; she'd called him for advice because he was someone she knew who was with the police force. But there was an intensity when Wilkinson's name was mentioned that made O'Mally wonder about this. O'Mally later recalled she 'formed the opinion whilst speaking with Kylie that she was lonely and may have been susceptible to mental health issues. I formed this opinion based on my experience interviewing numerous sexual assault victims and experience as a police negotiator.'

Still, Kylie was sticking to her story. O'Mally told her about counselling services she might like to contact and then passed the investigation over to City Central Police Station, because the alleged assault had occurred in the city. That night Kylie didn't sleep well. According to her diary, 'The statement was on my mind. The night kept going through my mind. It was like a nightmare, flash backs. I was home alone and [that] made me a little more frightened.' At this time Sean was often away, on the ship or working in Canberra. On 17 March Kylie had trouble sleeping once more, and the next day she wrote: 'dyed my hair burgundy as tomorrow is a month since sexual assault couldn't stand having blond hair any more as it reminded me of sexual assault.' On 23 March she wrote: 'Todd Holoson contacted me from City Central Police Station Darling Harbour re. case and progress. Todd to call me next week to make arrangements to come to station and discuss case.' This was the last diary entry of any substance about the rape.

Donna O'Mally must have been surprised to receive a phone call from Paul Wilkinson on 7 May. He said he had something to tell her about the rape, and later that day came to see her. He said Kylie had admitted to him that she'd made up the whole thing. In fact, she had been having an affair with Gary and was now pregnant by him, and had said she might move interstate to be with him. Wilkinson said Kylie's family had called him. (This was the day he received the phone calls from Michael and Leanne Edwards.)

O'Mally listened to this and thought there was something strange about Wilkinson's manner. He was uptight and 'appeared to be disjointed in his conversation and I was having trouble getting facts . . . from him'. She urged him to call Kylie's relatives and ask them to report her missing, and to tell Gosford police the report number for the sexual assault, and also to tell them about the possibility Kylie was with Gary. Wilkinson did this. O'Mally asked about his own connection with Kylie. He said they had not had a sexual relationship, but from his manner she suspected this was false.

Once Craig had obtained and read all the documents relevant to the alleged rape, she contacted Gary and asked if Kylie was with him. He said she wasn't. He hadn't seen her since the time they met in Sydney. He denied the rape allegation and was distressed by it. He had an alibi for the time she'd disappeared.

Rebekkah Craig wondered about the rape story. Donna O'Mally was an experienced officer; if she thought Kylie might be lying, that had to be taken seriously. But what possible reason could there be for such an extraordinary fabrication? And where did Paul Wilkinson fit in? In particular, what was to be made of his claim to have heard from Kylie in recent days, about going to live with Gary?

By the end of the first week of the investigation, Craig was pretty sure that neither Sean nor Gary was involved in Kylie's disappearance, which left one person of interest. She hoped to learn more when she interviewed Paul Wilkinson the following week.

When Craig arrived at work at 8.00 a.m. on Monday 17 May, there was a note on her desk asking her to contact Detective Mark Polley at Bankstown detectives. She called and heard yet another weird tale: there had been a fire at Paul Wilkinson's house in Picnic Point in Sydney's south. Wilkinson was claiming that one of those who'd set it was Kylie Labouchardiere, and that she'd tied him up and left him there, presumably in the hope he would burn to death. Fortunately, the fire had done only modest damage to the house, and Wilkinson had not been injured. Given the apparent seriousness of the incident, Bankstown police had driven up to Louisa Windeyer's flat to see if they could find Kylie. They'd learned of her disappearance and now wanted to talk with Craig to see if she'd found anything that might help them.

The case was becoming complicated, so Craig's senior officer, Detective Sergeant Peter Houlahan, decided he would accompany her to Bankstown to talk to the detectives there. He was to be the officer in charge of the investigation for the next year. The detectives drove to Sydney—the first of many long trips the investigation would require—where Mark Polley showed them the statement Wilkinson had provided after the fire.

Wilkinson was twenty-eight years old and lived in a rented house in Kelvin Parade with his wife, Julie Thurecht, and their six-month-old son, Bradley. It was a simple two-bedroom place, fibro with a tile roof, and a driveway running up the side. Late on Saturday afternoon, he'd left Julie and the child at her parents' home at nearby Illawong, just across the Georges River, and was driving to see his own parents at the Engadine RSL when his mobile rang. When he answered, all he heard was heavy breathing, and he hung up after about ten seconds. He then drove home because 'for the last couple of nights there had been an increase in vehicles travelling up and down the street', which was normally a very quiet one.

Wilkinson said that when he arrived he went into the lounge room, where he was confronted by Kylie, whom he knew as an acquaintance. He said they'd first met a few months earlier and that she'd told him she'd been raped. After urging her to report it to police, he had 'kept in contact with Kylie regarding the sexual assault and progress of the case. During this time Kylie started becoming possessive and would call me up to eight times a day. I didn't speak with Kylie all the time but did some of the time. Along with the phone calls Kylie would send me SMS messages. The messages saying that I was hers and that she wasn't getting on with her husband and wanted to be with me.' He said that after a while he had came to doubt the truth of the rape allegation, because Kylie would change the details every time she talked about it. Eventually, he had told her she was 'full of shit' and suggested she return to the police and admit she'd made a false statement.

'It wasn't long after this,' he said, 'that I heard Kylie was in fact having an affair with [Gary, who] was supposed to have sexually assaulted her.' Asked why Kylie might have made up the rape claim, he said, 'It's the easiest way to get a divorce, 'cause it would have put a rift through the family . . . her husband's side of the family [because they were close to Gary]'. According to Wilkinson, Kylie had continued to pester him, even coming to visit him at Marrickville Police Station, where he was then working, and where she stole some police property: a digital hand-held video recorder, a mobile phone and a number of portable two-way radios. The Marrickville crime manager spoke to Wilkinson about these thefts, and he had a word with Kylie and she returned the items.

After this she started sending him text messages of a sexual nature, even though he didn't want to have a sexual relationship with her. When he told her this, 'The messages and phone calls soon turned nasty, and I started to receive death threats in my mail,' he told police, 'along with messages from Kylie such as I was going to get my car blown up and that my wife and kid would be killed.'

Like many fantasists, Wilkinson sometimes included bits and pieces of the truth in his fabrications. In the above account, the story of Kylie visiting him at work might have been true: it recalls the visits she used to make to Sean's naval base. Wilkinson said he continued to receive threatening messages from Kylie until about 25 April (just a few days before she disappeared), when she told him she was going interstate to be with Gary. Wilkinson told her they first had to tell the police the rape allegation was false, and she agreed to come to Sutherland Railway Station on the night of 28 April. (He did not say why he had to be involved in this.) He said he'd driven there but she hadn't turned up, and he'd had no communication with her since that day, until he found her in his house on 16 May, along with a tall, thin Aboriginal man who looked about thirty years old and sported a moustache and a number-two haircut. Kylie was wearing a white short-sleeve shirt and blue track pants, and the man had a black jumper and black pants. Wilkinson had never seen him before. 'As soon as I saw both Kylie and the male standing in front of me,' Wilkinson told police, 'I thought they were there to hurt me in some way. I don't know how they got into the house as I [had] shut the front door behind me when I entered, they must have been there when I walked in. I have immediately struck out and punched Kylie in the mouth. At the same time of doing this the male with Kylie had punched me once above the right eye causing me to stumble backwards before falling over and landing on the floor. The man has yelled, "Black cunt. Is this the cunt?"

'Kylie said, "That's the fucking asshole." When I landed on the floor both Kylie and the male jumped on top of me. I have felt my hands being grabbed and they were bound with something in front of my body . . . it was also around my neck at the same time because I was restricted in movement, I couldn't move my hands very far. I was trying to pull my hands down and it was pulling my head down with me . . . The male then said to me, "What's this fucking stuff?" I didn't answer him as I didn't know what the fuck he was talking about. The male has then said [to Kylie], "Where did Mick say the evidence was?"'

This was a reference to Mick Hollingsworth, the Redfern police officer who had been driving the car when TJ Hickey died four months earlier, and who was blamed for the death by many Aboriginal people. The 'evidence' was Wilkinson's work notebook, in which he had recorded details of Kylie's changing stories about her alleged rape, an account of the theft of items from Marrickville Police Station, and a record of death threats he said he'd been receiving. Then, his account continued, Kylie said, 'Mick said [the notebook was] in the house.'

Wilkinson responded, 'I ain't got it, I've handed it in.' He said the man placed something like a jumper over his face, and he just lay there, too scared to move. He heard things being moved about the house and then the noise of the back door banging shut. There was the smell of smoke so he rolled over and managed to get to his feet, when the jumper fell off his face and he could see. He ran through the house, finding much of it alight and filled with smoke. He went into the main bedroom and closed the door to keep the smoke out, and then kicked the window out and yelled for help. No one came, so he clambered through the hole and ran to his neighbour's and knocked. When no one answered, he ran up the street knocking on doors until one opened. 'Ring the coppers and ring the firies,' he gasped. 'The house is on fire.' As a result of the incident, he said, 'I have a burning throat, it hurts slightly when I breathe, I have a shocking fucking headache and a lump above my right eye. I have sore wrists and my neck is a bit sore.'

After Houlahan and Craig read Wilkinson's statement, they asked Mark Polley what he thought. He was suspicious about the fire: the house doors were barricaded from the inside, which didn't fit Wilkinson's story; and there were the mystifying movements of Burt, a yellow Cockatiel pet that Wilkinson said had been in its cage in the kitchen when he entered the house. Yet the police had found it on the veranda, uninjured.

Craig agreed the fire was suspicious, and wondered why Wilkinson might have set it. One possibility was that he had killed Kylie in the house and was trying to destroy forensic evidence there. But the modest nature of the fire, which actually hadn't done a huge amount of damage, didn't strongly support that. She thought it more likely that, if he had killed her, the purpose of the fire was to throw the investigation off course by suggesting Kylie was still alive. If this was really what was going on, it was a distinctly curious way to do it, by turning himself into Kylie's victim.

Another interesting aspect of the story (which, as police suspected, was a complete fabrication—Wilkinson had set the fire himself) was the inclusion of a twisted version of the TJ Hickey case. This was the first of many times Wilkinson was to incorporate real events into his fantasies.

Once the Bankstown detectives had briefed Houlahan and Craig, they said they wanted to take over the investigation into Kylie's disappearance. This made a lot of sense because the focus was definitely in Sydney: Kylie had last been heard from at Central Station, the only person of interest was Paul Wilkinson of Picnic Point, and the fire there was probably linked to her disappearance. It was all a long way from the Coast. But the crime manager back at Gosford refused to give up the investigation, which is how it came to be run from such a distance over the next five years. Once this was resolved, Houlahan and Craig arranged to interview Wilkinson the next day.

While driving back to Gosford, Craig rang the Homicide Squad, which is based at Parramatta. Homicide does not handle all murders in New South Wales, but its specialist detectives are available to advise local detectives working murder investigations. This advice can cover everything from techniques of collecting evidence to how to go about obtaining the necessary resources. Craig said they needed advice—it was clear by now this would not be a straight-forward case—and was put on to Detective Inspector Andrew Waterman. Then in his forties, Waterman was one of the most experienced homicide investigators in the state. His successes included the arrests of serial killers such as Ivan Milat and John Glover, the so-called 'granny killer'. He lived on the Coast and was known and respected by many of the officers there, so Craig was pleased to learn his team was on call that day. She and Waterman had the first of what were to be many conversations about Paul Wilkinson.

One thing they discussed was how she and Houlahan should approach Wilkinson the next day. The problem was that although his behaviour on many counts was highly suspicious, they did not have one piece of firm evidence linking him to Kylie's disappearance. Because of this uncertainty, they would need to proceed with caution. Once Wilkinson realised he was a suspect, he would probably 'lawyer up' and be advised not to speak to the police anymore. It was decided, in order to minimise the chance of rattling him, to keep their approach fairly relaxed.

Craig's first interview with Paul Wilkinson took place on 18 May at Bankstown Police Station. He was pretty much as she remembered him: a good-looking, dark-skinned man of average build, although he'd put on some weight. In manner he was confident and talkative. Houlahan and Craig began the conversation by asking about his recent relationship with Kylie; they learned that, following previous encounters at Redfern and Miranda, Wilkinson and Kylie had met again when she'd been working as a nurse's aide at Sutherland Hospital. In December 2003 he'd gone into the hospital for a few days of tests.

While he was there, he said, 'I wasn't really allowed to smoke but I did, and I remember one time it was about half past three in the morning . . . I snuck out for a smoke . . . she came out to the smoking area and she put it on me there.'

'What did she say or do?' said Craig.

'She said, "We're alone," she put her hand on my genitals. I pulled away and I just got up and went to my ward.'

They'd kept in contact after Wilkinson left hospital, he said, partly because Kylie was interested in joining the police force, and partly because she wanted to have sex with him.

Wilkinson's behaviour during the interview was peculiar. Sometimes he'd try to dominate by asking his own questions. At several points he was even aggressive, saying things like, 'What are you asking that shit for?' and 'What are you, stupid?' He seemed particularly hostile towards Craig, which was odd because at Redfern they'd got on well enough, and Wilkinson had had a good relationship with her husband, who is also part-Aboriginal. Craig asked Wilkinson if Kylie had ever been in his car. He said she'd got in one time and refused to get out unless he 'engaged in some sort of sexual thing with her and I refused and refused and refused and it was at that point that she said to me she was going home to ask her husband for a threesome, her, her husband and myself. It frightened the shit out of me in the end.'

Craig asked if Kylie and he had eventually had sex. 'No . . . I just told her that I was married and I had a young bloke.'

'Did you ever think she had an obsession with you personally?'

'Yeah, she did . . . she had problems with her husband and she couldn't have children. She always said she wanted to have a copper's child or a dark child.'

'I got hit with two things from her,' he said in a long and rambling answer to a question about Kylie's problems. One was the alleged rape. The other was 'info about Mick and what happened with TJ'. Kylie had told him something important about Hollingsworth, although he wouldn't say what. 'I told her . . . she's gunna have to speak to someone who's in a very high position about TJ. She went, like, weird after that and, you know, and like I've never been frightened of anyone in my life, I'll stand there and have a crack at anyone. She had me that much in fear because, you know, she said she was gunna have me fixed, she was gunna inform my wife that we were having an affair, when we weren't having an affair. She threatened my family if I was to speak out about the sexual assault and the TJ incident. I was more or less like a puppy led around by her. My wife hasn't seen an angry man, she wouldn't know what an angry man is, she hasn't been around violence before.'

Craig listened with surprise to Wilkinson's convoluted, even disjointed, responses. This wasn't how he'd been back in their days at Redfern.

He went on, 'I was extremely frightened for my young bloke and should also add in there back, I'm yet to be investigated for it but I will at some stage. Items went missing from Marrickville Police Station and they were [the] crime co-ordinator's mobile phone, and one of those hand-held video cameras . . . it was Kylie, she was gunna, this is how she had me, it may even cost me my job. I mean if I was to say anything to the Marrickville commander, he was asking the initial questions, she was going to deny everything, I didn't know what to do, I have to bring money in for the young bloke, he is forever growing. I guess what I'm trying to say to you, Beck, is everything that is going on, she was the centre of it.'

The more Wilkinson talked, the more he said had been 'going on'. He said he'd received death threats, and Houlahan and Craig asked for details.

'About two months ago,' he recalled, 'my wife and I came home, I go through the same ritual when I come home. I walk inside the house first before my wife and kid come in. I've opened the front door and as you walk in there is one of my boy's teddy bears stuck to the wall with a knife through its throat. I've told Julie to grab me boy and go next door to Dorothy's and stay there until I say so. In searching the rest of the house, on my fridge in large letters were DIE, the house was clear and I went to get Julie to have a look. I've then told Julie to pack some of her stuff and stay with her parents until I say it's safe to come home. I didn't report it to the police because I, I, I don't know . . . I did, I did question Kylie about what happened, there was no words, there was a sly giggle.'

During this offbeat conversation, Wilkinson was rung several times by his wife, Julie, who was waiting outside. Finally he said he had to go and terminated the interview. This, the first of a number of statements Wilkinson was to make to police, is revealing in retrospect, although to Craig at the time it was more of a bizarre jumble. It contains most of the key preoccupations and fantasies that were to be elaborated in many of his later statements and conversations. One is the notion of Kylie as a sexual predator, another that she was violent and a thief, and yet another that she possessed secret information about the truth of TJ Hickey's death. Then there is Wilkinson's apparent concern for his family's safety, his professed love for his son and the fear that his wife might leave him if Kylie told her she and Paul were having an affair—even when they weren't. And finally there was the peculiar comment about his own capacity for violence ('My wife hasn't seen an angry man . . .'), which had nothing to do with anything else in the conversation.

The interview was continued two days later when he came back; this time it was filmed and recorded. This procedure, known as an ERISP (Electronically Recorded Interview with a Suspected Person), is, as the name implies, most commonly used for suspects, but it can also be used by police to create a record of important witness interviews. After explaining to Wilkinson that he was not under arrest and was free to go at any stage, the detectives returned to the threats against his life. Another example of these was a letter he'd received at home with his car's registration number on it along with the word 'tick' repeated a dozen times.

'It got to the point that before even getting in the car I'd look under the car,' he said, 'with the tick, tick, tick, tick about twelve times . . . I could only assume that it was a bomb.' He said the letter was handwritten, the same as another letter he'd received. That one had been put on his vehicle when he was visiting the Aboriginal Medical Service. This mentioned a police officer's name in relation to the death of TJ Hickey, and Wilkinson gave it to the Aboriginal Legal Service. Another letter received at home referred to his wife's colourful pyjamas, which Wilkinson sometimes wore when he went outside in the morning to adjust their faulty water main. 'One of the letters,' he said, 'it was along the lines of "Nice pyjamas", or something to that effect. That had me like a bit windy, that's why I told Julie she's got to take the little boy over to her mother's and stay there for a while, 'cause the only time they would have seen me in the pyjamas was when I'd gone out the front, and that was an indication to me that, you know, it's possible that people are around watching.'

The letters, he said, were not sent through the post: someone had hand-delivered them to the mailbox out front of their house. Asked if he had any idea who had sent them, Wilkinson said, 'At the time I was 100 per cent certain that it was the blackfellas, the local blacks down there at the Block [in Redfern], after what had happened to TJ . . . the day in which I went to the Aboriginal Medical Service . . . in the foyer there was not less than seven local Koori ladies, um, sheilas, and they gave me a hard time over what happened with TJ, and in the end when I was finished with the doctor I had to go out the back door because there was more of them down there, and that's when I've gone back to my car to go home and on the windscreen there was a letter.'

The officer named in this letter was Mick Hollingsworth. The detectives, recalling what Wilkinson had said earlier about his conversation with Kylie at Sutherland Hospital, asked how she had come to know of Hollingsworth's alleged responsibility for Hickey's death. 'They were knocking each other off [ie. having an affair],' Wilkinson said, 'Kylie informed me that . . . he told her [that he'd killed TJ Hickey], like, to her face . . . I put an entry in a notebook, um, and after that things just got nasty, where I was threatened, like, not to say anything . . . By Kylie, I was told not to say anything, otherwise harm would come to Julie, my wife, and Bradley my little boy.'

The detectives asked if he'd ever spoken to Hollingsworth

about TJ's death. He said he'd bumped into him at Red-fern Police Station on the afternoon after Hickey died, and Hollingsworth began to tell him how he'd 'put his hand through the wound in TJ's neck and placed it down towards his heart to stop the flow of blood'. But the conversation had been stopped by a senior officer, who Wilkinson said had come into the room and said to Hollingsworth, 'Don't fuckin' say anything in front of him.' (There is no evidence anything Wilkinson said about Michael Hollingsworth is true.)

Several times Houlahan and Craig pushed Wilkinson about the nature of his relationship with Kylie. He continued to deny having an affair with her and persisted with the story that she had pursued him and he had resisted but been too scared by her threats to just walk away. He said they'd exchanged maybe eight or ten SMS messages a day, and their content had been 'like a stage play, really, like, I was told what, you know, like, the messages she sent to me, in some of them were very sexual, like, I was told on what, you know, how to reply to it and I didn't dare go against what she said.' Asked for an example, he said, '"I want to suck your black cock", you know, you know, I had to reply like, "I want to pound your", like, I don't know if this is spot-on or not, but like, "I want to pound your white C-U-N-T".'

'And that's what you sent back?' said Craig.

'I was like a fuckin' dog cornered, like, you know . . . I was frightened of what would happen, not to me, so much to me, but my boy and my wife, you know, I was frightened and I'm frightened, I'm still frightened now.'

'And how many do you think of those sexual—'

Wilkinson said, 'Oh, you're talking thousands there.'

'A lot.'

'A hell of a lot.' Craig asked how he'd felt when Kylie threatened to lie to his wife and say they were having an affair. He said he didn't want her to do this: 'My wife, she's jealous of any woman in the world, I know what it's like when I drive the car down the street, I've got to put horse blinkers on if I look to the right or look to the left, I'm supposed to be, you know, possibly looking at someone's arse or someone's breasts. That's the reason I don't go down the academy any more and do any of the Aboriginal lecturing to the probies . . . it was in her head that I'd go down there and I'd sniff around the Eagles' Nest for a sheila . . . That's why I stopped going down there, anyone would think you're the world's fuckin' prettiest man, you know, the way she goes on.' (Probies are probationary constables; the Eagles' Nest referred to the academy bar—the eagle is the symbol of the NSW Police Force.)

Returning to Kylie, the detectives asked if she'd ever wanted him to leave his wife for her. 'Yeah,' he said, 'that was mentioned, she actually um, mentioned that, she would have Julie knocked off . . . have her killed, you know.'

Houlahan and Craig knew a bit about Kylie by now, from speaking to her family, her husband and some of her colleagues. They'd received no hint she was the sort of monster Wilkinson was describing. They wondered what it all meant, unaware that this particular fantasy—Kylie as a threat to Julie's life—would emerge years later as Wilkinson's justification for the murder he had committed less than a fortnight before this interview. But for now, they could only sit back and ask themselves what the hell he was raving about. They knew he was lying, but his lies were not mere denials, they were well-developed fantasies.

And the more he spoke, the more the fantasies grew. It was hard to keep on top of them all. 'I was frightened of her,' he said, 'I was frightened of Mick [Hollingsworth], you know. She said that she had, whilst living in Melbourne she, you know, she had associations there with, you know, with the underground down there. She said she had association with the Bankstown boys . . . Said [a relative] was a major drug dealer in the Bankstown area and he's, he had some rough and ready associates, you know, that could have things done, you know, no wonder I didn't fuckin' say anything about anything, you know.'

Houlahan asked if Kylie had ever said she was pregnant, and Wilkinson said she'd told him five weeks ago she was pregnant to Gary. 'That's when I started to get frightened too,' he said, 'cause she was going to tell, she was going, this was what was thrown at me, she was going to spread the obsession, runs wild, she was going to tell my wife that [we were] having an affair, second to that, like, the child was mine and, like, you know, fuckin', it definitely would have been fuckin' divorce, without even the chance of DNA, the wife would have just packed my little boy up and just taken off.' The last time he saw Kylie, he said, was at the Sydney Football Stadium on Monday 26 April 2004, when Souths played Canterbury. Wilkinson had insisted she tell the police her rape allegation was false, they had argued about this, and later she had agreed and arranged to meet him at Sutherland Railway Station on 28 April, to go to the local police station so she could retract her story about the rape. Wilkinson turned up on that evening, at about 9.00 p.m., but there was no sign of Kylie.

After this interview, Craig was convinced that Wilkinson had killed Kylie. The case was circumstantial, but strongly so. Wilkinson's behaviour and stories suggested someone who was trying to cover up a crime. He had sought to minimise his relationship with Kylie but the records showed otherwise. The detectives had now obtained details of all her phone use in the months before her disappearance, and the volume was staggering. There had been 23,836 phone calls and text messages between Wilkinson and her from 21 December 2003 to 28 April 2004—an astonishing average of 184 per day. His claim that there had been only eight or ten calls a day was nonsense. It was self-defeating nonsense, though, because he must have known this was something that could and would be easily checked. But then, as Craig now knew, Paul Wilkinson was a peculiar man. He wasn't stupid but he was lazy; probably, he just hadn't thought things through.

A police analyst set to work on the telephone data, and patiently pieced together all the calls for 28 April, showing Kylie and Wilkinson had been in frequent contact. The analyst noted the mobile phone towers used by the phones for each call, as these indicate the general location of a mobile at the time a call is made or received. They suggested that for most of the day, Wilkinson had been at home in Picnic Point and Kylie at her grandmother's place in Erina. Then Kylie left Erina and caught the train, and by 8.00 p.m. her calls were using a city tower as she approached Central Station. At 9.10 p.m. she made a call using the Sutherland tower, and Wilkinson's phone received it using the tower at Bonnet Bay, in between Picnic Point and Sutherland. This suggests she had changed trains at Central and was on her way to Sutherland, and that he was driving to the station to collect her. Soon after, Kylie called him again and both their phones used the Sutherland tower, indicating they were very close. And yet, according to Wilkinson, he arrived at the station and she wasn't there.

If this is really what had happened, you'd expect one of them would have rung the other to find out what was happening. But there were no more phone conversations between them that evening. What the records showed is exactly what would have happened if they had met successfully at Sutherland.

Once the police had the phone records and realised Kylie must have taken the train to Sutherland, they tried to obtain CCTV footage from the station. Unfortunately, it retained footage for only fourteen days, and more than that time had now passed since Kylie's disappearance.

According to the phone records, there had been no more activity from either phone until 10.15 p.m., when Wilkinson rang his uncle Alan Wilkinson, who lives on Mooney Mooney Creek beneath the F3 bridge of that name. This call was made using the Picnic Point tower, suggesting that Wilkinson had gone back home from Sutherland Station. Forty minutes later, there was a text from Kylie's phone to Sean Labouchardiere, also using the Picnic Point tower, and two texts from Wilkinson's phone to Kylie's. Wilkinson was called by his cousin Brigette Fernando at 10.54 p.m., and there was one last intriguing text for the day: from Kylie's phone to that of Gary, the man she'd said had raped her. This time, Kylie's phone was using the tower at Illawong. The detectives were deeply suspicious of this pattern of activity.

The Text Trail: communication between Paul Wilkinson and Kylie Labouchardiere on 28 April 2004 showing locations of mobile phone towers

Kylie Labouchardiere	Time	Paul Wilkinson
Gosford	1.17 am	Picnic Point
Gosford	2.56 pm	Illawong
Gosford CBD	6.36 pm	Revesby Heights
Central	8.15 pm	Picnic Point
Central	8.31 pm	Heathcote Road
Surry Hills	8.39 pm	Heathcote Road
Sutherland	9.10 pm	Bonnet Bay
Sutherland	9.11 pm	Sutherland

Source: Chart prepared by an intelligence analyst for Strike Force Bergin

On the day Kylie Labouchardiere disappeared, 74 calls and text messages were exchanged between her phone and Wilkinson's. Phone records showed police which mobile phone towers had been used by each of their phones at different times of the day, thereby indicating their locations. The above list indicates the times of the day at which the tower in use (and therefore the person's location) changed. Wilkinson initially denied meeting Kylie's train at Sutherland that night, but the records suggest otherwise: he left home at Picnic Point soon after 8.15 pm and was in the vicinity of the railway station when she arrived.

When put in the context of the frequency of phone communication between Kylie and Wilkinson over the previous months, it suggested the two had met up after 9.00 p.m. and had not separated afterwards. Wilkinson might have sent a few text messages from Kylie's phone later that night to create the impression she was still alive.

The investigation continued in other areas. A search warrant was executed on the Erina Medical Centre, which confirmed it had conducted a positive pregnancy test on Kylie on 13 April and estimated she was five weeks pregnant. Formal statements were taken from Kylie's mother and grandmother. Carol said Kylie had never run away before, and she'd always kept in close contact with her grandmother by phone. Both women agreed that Kylie's continuing silence was completely out of character. On 25 May 2004, Craig and Houlahan met with Andrew Waterman to discuss the progress of the investigation. By now it had a name, generated at random by a computer: Strike Force Bergin.

The next day the detectives visited Sutherland with photos of Kylie, to see if anyone remembered seeing her. Sutherland, the urban centre of the Shire, is one of those places that looks bigger on the map than in reality. The railway station where Kylie had come on the night she disappeared is an old place painted in pleasant light colours. You ascend the steps from the platform to the road that crosses the station on a bridge, and then go in either direction over the line and down to a strip of largely unrenovated older shops. It's a quiet place where it would be very difficult to miss anyone coming off the train, if you were waiting for them. But few people would have been there at that time of night, and no one recalled seeing Kylie.

The detectives visited Kelvin Parade in Picnic Point and canvassed the houses there to see if anyone recalled Kylie from the day of Wilkinson's house fire. These inquiries also drew blank. A big question was where Wilkinson might have killed Kylie. The house was examined for forensic evidence but yielded nothing.

On 2 June the detectives went to Wilkinson's parents' house, in Yarrawarrah in southern Sydney, where Julie, Bradley and he had been living since the fire, and executed a search warrant for the car he used. Wilkinson called Legal Aid while Craig told Julie, 'We're just going to be seizing this vehicle and having it forensically examined as I've explained to Paul already, okay? . . . You can have the vehicle back in twenty-four hours, so tomorrow morning you'll be able to pick it up.'

Wilkinson asked why they were interested in the car and Craig said, 'You've admitted Kylie was in it.'

Julie heard this comment and it was news to her. She knew Kylie was missing and her husband had had professional deal-ings with her—but why had she been in their car? She grabbed the baby seat from the car and stormed off. Later she had an argument with Paul who, far from apologising, was upset by her behaviour, which he thought made him look guilty.

For the first time, Julie realised Paul was a person of inter-est in the police investigation. She told her parents, Kevin and Jenene Thurecht, who discussed it with Paul. He told them Kylie had been in the car once because she'd been try-ing to persuade him to hand over his notebook containing incriminating information about her drug-dealing lover Mick Hollingsworth. For the moment they believed him: he had always exaggerated the excitement and importance of his work at Redfern, so as far as they were concerned, these new stories were plausible. The Thurechts would come to realise that Paul was a thorough fantasist and had lied to them almost continually, but it was to be a long and gradual awakening.

The car was taken to the Sydney Police Centre in Surry Hills and fingerprinted and examined. There wasn't much there, apart from various receipts and other bits of paper. The Crime Scene people removed a hair and some unspecified debris from the mat in the boot. When the examination was finished, a woman from Clean Scene came to clean the vehicle so it could be returned to its owners. She found a stain on a front seat, and a section of it was cut out for analysis. The next day Wilkinson called Craig at 9.15 a.m. to ask when he could have the car back. She explained they'd taken a piece from the seat but would replace it. 'Why?' said Wilkinson. 'What did you find?'

'Well, we've found something on the seat and we've had to take it.'

'No,' he said, 'that's not what I asked you. What did you find on the seat?'

Again Craig was struck by his arrogance. 'Well, I'm not prepared to tell you at this stage,' she said. 'We're going to have it analysed. Don't worry about the seat—we will have it replaced. We should be able to get it back to you within an hour at the most.'

In the end, the car provided no forensic evidence of Kylie. In fact, from this point on, the investigation began to run down. Craig had strong suspicions about Wilkinson but no proof, and most of her inquiries ran into dead ends. In July she talked with Maxine Cahill, the woman who'd helped bring up Kylie, and went to Dubbo to examine Kylie's possessions, which were still in Ark Self Storage, where the removalists had left them on 29 April. The items provided no suggestions as to what had become of her. In September, the detectives talked to an official at the Centre for Mental Health about the possibility that Kylie might have admitted herself into a psychiatric hospital, where patients' details are kept secret. There is no central register of such patients, so the detectives contacted thirty-two hospitals around the state. The response was non-conclusive: twenty did not reply. (A more success-ful search was conducted later, but it too found no trace of Kylie.)

The detectives asked to see the death threats Wilkinson said he'd received, and gave the letters and envelopes, along with a sample of Kylie's handwriting, to an expert docu-ment examiner in the police Forensic Services Group. He compared elements of the writing such as slant, spacing, connections and pen lifts, and came to an important conclu-sion: Kylie had definitely written one of the items, and had probably written five others. On several occasions Wilkinson had sent Julie and Bradley to her parents to stay for a while after receiving these death threats. The discovery they'd been written by Kylie suggested that their purpose had been to get Julie out of the way so they could have an affair.

And yet despite all this, despite knowing Paul Wilkinson was a chronic liar, there was still not one scrap of physical evidence as to how Kylie might have disappeared or died. For the detectives, it was deeply frustrating. The investiga-tion continued throughout the second half of 2004, with

Craig and Houlahan doing what they could, along with all their other duties. But gradually, due to the lack of anything firm, it wound down. Gosford is a busy police station, and before long it became difficult to justify spending much time on Kylie's investigation, given it was going nowhere and there were so many other new crimes that needed their attention.

Most murders are solved fairly soon after they are committed, or not at all. If Paul Wilkinson was a killer, it was starting to look as though he'd got away with it.

Meanwhile, the Edwards family were distraught. They had been told almost nothing of what the detectives were doing. This is standard: most investigations involve uncovering information of a private nature, and the police are not allowed by law to disclose any of this to third parties. Apart from privacy issues, there's concern about what a victim's family might do if they learned the identity of someone who was suspected (possibly incorrectly) of being the murderer. But this was no consolation to the Edwards as the weeks and months passed by.

In the second half of 2004, Carol Edwards was constantly on the phone to Gosford Police Station, emotional and demanding information. Her grief was tinged with the memory of her last conversation with Kylie. 'What are you planning to do with your life?' Carol had demanded.

Kylie had refused to say and they'd argued; Kylie had left without saying goodbye. Now Carol thought about this every day, wishing she could take back those last words.

Although John was not as emotional as Carol in his dealings with the police, he took the lack of information very hard. As far as the family knew at this point, Paul Wilkinson was a serving police officer, and several of the detectives in the investigation had served with him at Redfern. Some of the family started to wonder if the New South Wales Police Service might be protecting one of its own. John decided to deal with his suspicions by commencing his own investigation. He had a certain amount of experience to guide him: he'd served in the army for twenty years, in Australia and Asia, and retired as a Warrant Officer Class One, Supervisor Communications for Australia.

For a while he worked twenty hours a day, going through every detail on every piece of paper of Kylie's he could find, trying to build a picture of her life in the months before her disappearance. Like the police, he found she'd exchanged an extraordinary number of text messages with Paul Wilkinson. There was one period of several days when he couldn't see how she could have slept, because by his calculation there had been a call at least once every five minutes. Based largely on his daughter's diaries and phone records, he prepared an analytical profile of her movements and phone calls from 18 January 2003, when she had married Sean, until the time she disappeared.

He found that her diaries were generally just a record of things done and didn't indicate her state of mind. There was almost no reference to Wilkinson, and in fact her diary for the current year suggested her marriage had been going well. On 17 January 2004, Sean took her on a Captain Cook cruise on Sydney Harbour for their first wedding anniversary, an event she described as 'wonderful'. On Australia Day the couple went to the Garden Island naval base and inspected a submarine.

'It was fantastic,' she recorded, 'so confined and so many levels. I wouldn't join though not for me at all.' On Valentine's Day, she 'gave Sean his gift first thing in morning. Sean then went to Miranda to buy me a gift. I got a big love bear-shaped balloon a teddy and a card. This night we got dressed up and drove to the city and had dinner at Centrepoint Revolving Restaurant. The view was magnificent. It was a sunny clear day. The restaurant revolved four times prior to our departure.'

Possibly the diary entries had been made on the assumption that Sean might read them. The phone records, with her incessant communication with Wilkinson, painted a very different picture of her life at the time: they even revealed that she had phoned him from Centrepoint Tower while she was there with Sean on Valentine's Day. John tried to find out more from people who'd known Kylie, and discovered from her address book that she'd actually had few friends. The one he did speak with was Maxine Cahill, whom the detectives also talked to. She told him that on 5 February Kylie had visited and said she was moving to the country with a policeman. Kylie had been texting the man all the time she was with Maxine, and said she'd been having problems with Sean, who was accusing her of having an affair.

During his investigation, John read documents, listened to tapes, looked at photographs and talked to people. The experience was sometimes overwhelming, and he would have to take a few days off before immersing himself once more in

Kylie's life. Finally he compiled all his information into a report and sent it to the Gosford detectives. He tried contacting them often but was not always successful, and became increasingly angry at what he saw as a lack of communication. A few email responses from Peter Houlahan, received after John had provided him with an updated version of the analytical report, give a flavour of what he was going through, as well as the pressure of the other work the detectives were performing.

Houlahan and Craig had been looking into a possible sighting of Kylie in Dubbo. On 10 June 2004 Houlahan emailed, in part, 'I don't feel it is Kylie, but possibly someone who looks remarkably like her. I sent another request to the Crime Manager at Dubbo yesterday afternoon asking him to treat our request as a priority bearing in mind that they had a murder there on Tuesday evening. I will keep you advised.'

And on 1 July 2004: 'Unfortunately some of the strategies we are currently employing are covert and as such what I can tell you is quite limited at this time. I can however assure you that we have not lost sight of the importance of this investigation and will continue to diligently pursue all avenues of inquiry in an effort to locate Kylie.'

John continued with his own investigation. He would go to work in the daytime and come home and do what he could to find out more about Kylie's life in the months before she disappeared. Gradually, he filled in bits of the picture. Some pieces of paper found in Kylie's room were particularly interesting. One was a list of thirty questions in her handwriting, apparently intended for Paul Wilkinson. It is undated but would have been written not long before her disappearance. 'When are you going to tell your family about us?' was one, and another read: 'When are you going to leave Julie?' According to another: 'A couple of weeks ago I asked you to separate 10 balls all worth 10 per cent. What is it now? 80/20 Kylie-Julie.'

The last line read: 'Paul if you say you love me as much as you do I need to see it.'

By this time John had found out that Wilkinson was not a police officer. It was possible he'd intended to retrain as one, though: the questions on the list suggest he and Kylie were planning to go to the Goulburn Police Academy together (or that he'd lied to her that was his intention). They also reveal her high level of dependence on Wilkinson; for example, she'd accepted his request not to tell her family about him. Several others indicated that he was involved with some police unit called 'the team', and that Kylie wanted to join it too. Some of the questions suggest a certain ignorance of the world. Kylie asks, for instance, if she will have to pay for her own police uniform, and if 'the DPP will cost me anything'. The last reference is probably to the Office of the Director of Public Prosecutions, the government agency that would have prosecuted Gary if the rape case had ever gone to trial.

Putting it all together, John realised that Kylie had not been as happy as he'd thought when the family had had dinner with Sean and her on New Year's Eve. In fact, her marriage had been falling to pieces; the only thing keeping her in it appeared to be Wilkinson's reluctance to leave his wife for her. John discovered a sad reflection of this in conflicting notices Kylie had placed in the *Daily Telegraph* on Valentine's Day, two months before her disappearance. One read:

SEAN: 'Happy Valentine's Day! I love you with all of my heart and can't wait for you to come back home. Love always Bun Buns.'

The other:

PAUL: 'Happy Valentine's Day! Thank you for always being there for me. I know that there is a future for us and I can't wait to spend it with you. I love you and always will. Love SV69.'

In September 2004, to the surprise of many looking into Kylie's disappearance, Paul Wilkinson appeared in the media. He had volunteered to give evidence before the New South Wales Parliament's Standing Committee on Social Issues, which was investigating the Redfern Riots. Given his experience in the ACLO job, which he'd begun in 1997, and his familiarity with Redfern, he was potentially a valuable witness.

He claimed to be TJ Hickey's cousin and painted a picture of himself as a man well respected in the Aboriginal community. 'I socialise in Redfern,' he told the members of parliament. 'I feel safer in Redfern and Waterloo than I do anywhere else in Sydney . . . I played footy with various kids' fathers who are now in trouble with the police . . . I went to preschool in Redfern.'

But the role of Aboriginal Community Liaison Officer brought tension with it: 'In our job, basically, the community wants you to be on their side . . . and the police expect you to be on their side.'

Regarding the death of TJ Hickey, Wilkinson declared there had been a cover-up. He said the police car driven by Mick Hollingsworth had rammed Hickey and directly caused his death. It was a sensational claim, and there was more, for Wilkinson said pressure had been put on him to keep quiet about what he knew. 'I've had me house burnt down as a result of the crap that's gone on, I've had death threats stating to stay away from this inquiry,' he said. 'And you may ask who from? The police.'

Wilkinson was not just wrong about what had happened to TJ Hickey, he was inventing stories to support his version of events. He seemed to have decided to set himself in opposition to the police and portray himself as a victim, a tendency that was to increase in the coming years. Just why he went down this path is impossible to say with certainty, although potential reasons will emerge later in this story. I have been unable to ask him myself, as writers are not allowed to interview inmates in New South Wales prisons.

One factor possibly related to his craving for the status of victim, noted by some who knew him, was his laziness. He had a deep dislike of any sort of work, and it's possible the cause of the fights he picked with his employer was simply a desire to justify taking time off. In 1999 he claimed to have been stabbed with a blood-filled syringe, and even though the police force refused to believe him, he later said he'd had eight months' paid leave as a result. In October 2001 he was bitten on the hand by a prisoner—his wife, Julie, says the bite marks were barely visible a few hours later—and took twelve months' paid stress leave. He was on sick leave for other reasons from November 2003 to February 2004. Then—six months before he gave evidence to the parliamentary committee—he left his job and never worked again.

Work is the source of status and respect for most men, so abandoning it indicates an unusual preparedness to walk away from those things, and an acceptance of the further loss of status that comes from living on welfare unnecessarily. Circles of acquaintance dwindle and change, and in young men the lack of productive activity to fill the days often leads to tension with family and crime and violence as an outlet for frustrated energy. Male murderers are far more likely than men in general to be unemployed.

In any case, Wilkinson's evidence to the parliamentary inquiry was sensational and it was published in the newspapers. One who read it with great attention was John Edwards. The parliamentary committee did not accept Wilkinson's version of events in its report, but John wondered if he might be right. Maybe Kylie was involved in some sort of police cover-up? John didn't know what to believe. He later admitted that in this long period, through 2004 and into 2005, he was consumed by grief and anger and was not thinking clearly. He continued to pore over the extensive coverage of the Redfern Riots and their aftermath, wondering if they held the secret to his daughter's disappearance.

Eventually, he formed the view that the police had lied about what had happened at Redfern (several officers were very forgetful during a subsequent investigation). He wondered if Kylie might have learned the truth from Wilkinson, possibly by accident, and whether she had been killed to keep her quiet. Leanne told him that Kylie had called her in early 2004 and asked if she knew any police officers she could really trust, because she had some information about dishonest police she needed to pass on.

Another of John's speculations was that Wilkinson might have killed Kylie for some other reason, and was being protected by police in return for his silence over what he knew about the death of TJ Hickey. This didn't make much sense, but John was now living with three confusing nightmares. One was the simple fact of Kylie's disappearance. Then there was the police silence and the strange nature of the little he did know, such as the alleged rape and Wilkinson's story about Kylie burning down his house. On top of all this, there were now the conspiracy theories John's fevered mind was building.

'I was starting to go crazy,' he later admitted. 'I really needed to pull back, for my own sanity.' But he didn't know that then. Not the least of his problems was that, despite some of his theories, he still couldn't believe in his heart that Kylie was dead.

By the end of 2004, the police investigation had almost stopped. Houlahan and Craig had reached a dead end, convinced Wilkinson was a killer but, despite months of looking, lacking firm evidence they could take to court to support a charge of murder. Their bosses were no longer prepared to let them put time into an investigation that had already consumed a lot of resources but was going nowhere. Craig had the feeling that Wilkinson was slipping away from them.

Christmas 2004 was a sad time for the Edwards family, with everyone remembering the party they'd had at Kylie's the year before. Carol and John were shattered, desperately trying to maintain hope that their younger daughter was still alive. John spent Christmas alone, crying as he looked through photographs of the children when they were growing up.

'I felt so ashamed of myself for not being there for Kylie over all the years,' he says. 'I wanted to be able to let her know that I was sorry for not being a normal father to her. I remember praying to God to take good care of her, wherever she might be, and to forgive me.'

Carol was suffering depression. Leanne had to struggle to tell her young daughters why their aunty was no longer part of their lives. Michael had become unable to focus on his life and gave up his spot in a team in the Newcastle Premier League. Kylie's disappearance was tearing apart the lives of those left behind.

THE HUSBAND

Sean thought Kylie had done an excellent job arranging their wedding in February 2003: everyone said it was the most organised wedding they'd been to. She had also organised their work-related moves since they'd been living together, and he was impressed by this too, her ability to set herself up in a new area so easily. In retrospect, maybe it hinted at a certain lack of stability, an unusual capacity to detach herself from her surroundings and move on, but at the time he was just grateful.

Not long after the wedding her Bell's palsy recurred: Sean came home from work one day and saw one side of her face had dropped. They walked to a local doctor, who gave her some medication.

Over the next month or so, Kylie grew moody. Sean asked her what was wrong and she told him there was nothing to be planned any more, nothing to be achieved. She started to look around for another goal, and they talked about having children. Sean wondered if it was too soon, but Kylie became very keen. Before they'd even agreed to try to have a baby, she'd bought a cot and fitted out an entire nursery in their Melbourne home, complete with clothes and powders and lotions. It was, Sean thought, an example of her love of organisation. It was also an example of how marriage had done little to reduce her inability to compromise. According to John, she was very disappointed when she didn't fall pregnant during the following months.

Sean became a little concerned about Kylie's solitary nature. Being independent was one thing, but she took it too far. He knew it must be difficult when he was away at sea, and urged her to make some more friends, explaining how it was important to build up her own social life. She said she found this hard. One reason was that she was a strong-willed personality who wanted her own way, and she had little experience of the concessions and pleasantries needed to socialise successfully. When she encountered difficulty in relationships she often just walked away, rather than trying to work them out.

This was certainly the case at work. She was on the books of a job agency but none of the positions she took lasted very long. After a while Sean saw a pattern: Kylie would always be hugely enthusiastic about a new position and the people there, and offer to do night shifts and other unpopular work, which would impress her workmates. But after a few weeks, something always went wrong. Usually it involved a clash with a supervisor, when Kylie would take some comment the wrong way—she was oversensitive to criticism—and speak her mind. Sometimes there would be conflict with other colleagues too. At around the one-month mark, the job would become intolerable and Kylie would move on. She failed to make any lasting friendships at work.

Towards the end of the year, Sean was posted to HMAS *Newcastle*, and the couple moved back to Sydney. He was often away at sea, and he became more concerned at Kylie's isolation. When they were together she was the dominant person, and yet she had almost no life outside their marriage, wanting to spend all her time with him. While he was away she seemed to do nothing at all, as though her life was on hold. Although she didn't visit him at work as she had before, she still wanted to be with him as much as possible. When the ship sailed in to Garden Island, Sydney's main naval base, Sean would see her sitting on the wharf, waiting for him. This was unusual: wives weren't supposed to be on the base, but Kylie was able to sweet-talk her way past the guards. Sean found this irregular, although he also thought it was a bit of a compliment that Kylie wanted to be with him so much.

His colleagues found it irregular too. Kylie often called him at work for long conversations. She would also discover which bars he went to with male friends and turn up. For a while he had a female boss, and Kylie became intensely jealous, telling him she didn't like him working with this woman. One day when the ship came in, Kylie as usual was on the wharf watching. That night she told Sean he'd been standing too close to his boss on deck.

Despite Kylie's sometimes odd behaviour and lack of friends, Sean recalls 2003 as a good year. There was the holiday in Tasmania, the wedding and the move to Sydney to occupy their minds, and Kylie had decided to study nursing the next year, which gave her a new goal. The marriage appeared to him to be going well. They continued to enjoy each other's company, and would often go out to the back yard and kick a soccer ball around, wrestle and have a laugh. They had few arguments, and the ones they did have were soon over.

Carol liked Sean and thought the marriage was good for Kylie, who had gone through a rough time after the armed hold-up at the bowling club but now seemed to have turned some kind of corner. She was beautiful and kind, Carol says now, 'and I think it made her happy too that I was settled . . . While I was with Robert she used to worry I'd be killed, I wouldn't be around to see her get married. She was glad she'd got me out of that relationship and I was settled up on the Coast.'

The couple were living in a townhouse provided by the navy at Sylvania. Kylie was a keen housekeeper, almost obsessively so. Leanne noticed when she visited that the place was spotless and everything in it precisely placed, as though with the help of a ruler.

Kylie got a job as a nurse's aide at Sutherland Hospital, not too far away. This followed the usual pattern. At first she loved the place and often worked double shifts. Tina Kulevska was a nursing unit manager at the hospital. She later told police that the twenty-three-year-old Kylie struck her as looking 'quite young, but when you spoke to her you realised she had done quite a bit. Everyone seemed to get along with her [at first] and there were no dramas, if you asked for help she would help straight away without complaining. She seemed like a really nice person.' Kylie told Kulevska that some of her family had suffered from depression, but she seemed cheerful and content during her first weeks at the hospital in late 2003.

The first indication Sean had that something was wrong occurred one night in December 2003. He doesn't recall the exact date, but it was probably soon after Kylie met Paul Wilkinson when he was a patient at Sutherland Hospital. Kylie had been out without Sean, apparently to a hospital Christmas function at Cronulla, and when she came home he asked how it had been. She exploded in anger and accused him of suspecting her of cheating on him, something he had never considered.

From that night on, he says, the anger never really went away. If he asked a question about what she'd been doing, no matter how innocent, Kylie would accuse him of suspecting she was unfaithful. She began to send and receive a lot of text messages, and she refused to say who they were to and from. Some people would have been suspicious of all this, but Sean seems to have been an unusually trusting man. For a long time he was simply puzzled and upset by the changes in his wife's behaviour.

There's a photo from this time of Kylie and some of her nursing colleagues, all wearing their scrubs. She stands out, and it's not just because we know what was to happen to her. It's because of her grin, the nervous uncertainty of it, as though she half-expected to be caught out for something she'd done. Smiling but knowing she doesn't really deserve to be happy.

After Christmas, Sean found her distant and increasingly aggressive. It was as though she'd had some sort of personality change. She was often angry, yelling and swearing. On 19 January, on the Captain Cook cruise on Sydney Harbour to celebrate his birthday, he told her he might be posted interstate. It was just another piece of navy news, another move in a job full of them. But this time her reaction was very different to before, when she'd been excited about the prospect of change. She refused to contemplate leaving Sydney, saying she had family and friends here. When he asked who these friends were, she didn't reply. She talked about a police officer she'd nursed at Sutherland Hospital recently, and she seemed to have acquired an increased interest in police work. He asked if the new friends were police but she denied it vehemently.

Kylie began leaving the house suddenly in response to text messages. It might be during the day or at ten at night. When she returned, Sean would ask where she'd been and she wouldn't tell him. She'd just sit down and have a meal or jump into the shower and get changed for bed, as though nothing had happened. She also took up smoking, something she'd never done before. In fact, until then she hadn't even liked being around people who smoked. But now she began to light a new cigarette the moment the last one was out. Sean didn't smoke and didn't want the smell in the house, so Kylie would be outside most of the time, in the back yard with a smoke and her mobile phone. In the period of not much more than a month, their marriage had turned upside down.

Sean began to press harder for an explanation of why she'd

changed. At one point she told him she'd seen her old boy-friend Troy Myers recently. He asked if she was having an affair with anyone. She denied this and became even more angry. Finally, she told him she'd become friendly with a group of undercover police officers and was helping them with their work. Sean told her this sounded unusual and said he'd have a word with a cop he knew. Kylie exploded and insisted he say nothing, because that would get the officers she was working with in trouble: they reported directly to an assistant commissioner under a secret arrangement.

Today, Sean thinks Wilkinson must have seen how interested Kylie was in police work and lied to her about his own involvement in order to attract her to him. This, he believes, would have lured her 'hook, line and sinker'. In the days when she'd first been attracted to Sean himself, she'd developed a similar fascination with the navy. He suspects the stories she told him were based on a genuine belief that Wilkinson was engaged in some sort of important secret police work.

Sean, who seems to have been the most patient of men, decided not to make the inquiry. He didn't have much understanding of how the police worked and says he didn't realise at the time just how implausible his wife's stories were.

Some time in January 2004, Kylie rang her friend Maxine Cahill and asked if she could come over. When Kylie arrived she seemed agitated and was continually receiving and sending text messages. She said she wanted to catch up with her old school friends but after only twenty minutes announced that she had to go.

A fortnight later she turned up at Maxine's house again,

wearing the volunteer ambulance uniform she'd had at school. Maxine asked about this and Kylie said she'd wanted to put it on because it made her feel good. On this occasion, Kylie stayed with Maxine for a couple of hours, and she came back in early February for another chat. This time she said she'd developed feelings for a guy who worked in the police service; he was the person who was always texting her. They were planning to go away to Dubbo to live because he had relatives out there. This was dramatic stuff, especially as Kylie and Sean had been married only a year. Lots of marriages fall apart, of course, but rarely so soon. And then there was the idea of moving to Dubbo, so very different to anywhere Kylie had lived before. Maxine wondered what was going through Kylie's mind, what the reason for the sudden change could be, but it was impossible to work out. She wondered what had happened to her old friend, who as a teenager had been happy, often laughing. Now she seemed like a woman on the edge of a breakdown, agitated and nervous. And always texting.

Sean noticed another change in Kylie: a new passion for the South Sydney Rabbitohs rugby league team. When the season began, she started going to games, apparently by herself, and bought a sticker of a leaping bunny for their car. There were other changes too, in what she did and how she looked: she even wore her hair short for a while. By this point it was almost a relief for Sean to go to sea, which he did for periods of up to a few weeks. He was worried about Kylie and what she might be doing while he was away, but being at home didn't help anyway.

It was a bizarre life they were leading by now and Sean

became more disturbed. But he didn't know what to do: whenever he tried to talk to Kylie about it, she would get angry and tell him nothing, or else ramp up the level of drama. One day she announced that their lives were in danger but she couldn't guarantee his safety if she told him what was going on. She insisted again that he not make any inquiries into her police activities, as this would put them in more danger. It was crazy stuff. Later, John Edwards would resent the fact that Sean hadn't told the family what was happening. Sean seems to have felt it was something the couple needed to work out between themselves.

Some time in January 2004, Kylie called her boss, Tina Kulevska, to say her husband had announced he was leaving her. 'Kylie was very upset,' Kulevska later recalled to the police. 'She thought the world of him. She said she wanted to discuss it with him and he said he didn't want to discuss anything with her and it was over. I think at this stage she was still sending and receiving text messages, I don't know who she was texting.'

In fact, Sean had not said he was leaving her. Presumably Kylie had started to think about leaving him but preferred to present this to others by posing as the victim. Kulevska and another nurse took her out for dinner at a Thai restaurant, where they were struck by her odd appearance and behaviour. Normally, Kylie dressed conventionally, in casual clothes and without much makeup or jewellery. She had a gold charm bracelet with an anchor on it, and a few simple gold necklaces she sometimes wore when going out, but that was about it. On this occasion, though, 'she was dressed right up,' Kulevska recalls. 'She was wearing a lot of makeup and I thought she had gone off the rails. The makeup made her look like a psychiatric patient, with bright eye-shadow, bright lipstick, and her hair was done up.'

Kylie said her husband had asked where she was going and she'd told him she was going out—and what did he care anyway? During the meal, she received and sent text messages, holding her phone under the table, and also went out of the restaurant to answer phone calls.

After this, Kylie's behaviour at work grew more aberrant. 'She was scattered, she couldn't get it together or manage a shift,' Kulevska told police. 'She still got some of her work done but she was struggling to cope. Her behaviour was over the top. For example, if she saw me she would come up to me, very happy to see me, and give me a hug, which was very manic.'

On 22 January, Kulevska arranged for Kylie to see Lynne Baker, the hospital's employee counsellor. Normally, records of patient interviews with mental-health experts are confidential. In Kylie's case, some of them became part of the Crown's case against Paul Wilkinson, which is why they are now on the public record.

Kylie walked in to Baker's office and said, 'I'm suicidal.' She said she was having marital problems and demanded to be admitted to a psychiatric unit, and then asked that Kulevska come and sit with her.

When Kulevska arrived, Kylie looked unkempt and was crying a lot, plainly very upset. She said her family blamed her for the marriage breakdown and she wanted to jump off a bridge and end it all. Baker and Kulevska talked about her being admitted to a psychiatric ward, and she said she'd been in one when she was living in Melbourne. She kept crying and sobbing.

A few hours later, Kylie was seen by Dr Jarrett Johnston, the psychiatric registrar. She had calmed down and was lounging in her chair. The psychiatrist found her co-operative but sometimes evasive. She said she smoked ten cigarettes a day and two or three cones of marijuana. Her marriage was in trouble due to verbal abuse from her husband. She said she and Sean had not had sex for three months, and that she had been having an affair for one month. She had become irritable, had a poor appetite and was waking up during the night.

For several days she'd been feeling suicidal because her lover had been demoted at work 'because of acts of poor judgement related to me'. She said this made her feel guilty, and she was also not sure just how serious he was about their relationship. She had begun to drive recklessly. Johnston's conclusions were that Kylie tended to talk around the point and showed poor problem-solving skills. Her insight and judgement were poor and she minimised the seriousness of her choices. She said she felt helpless and trapped in her current domestic situation. However, she had 'no loosening of associations that would indicate more serious thought disorder'.

Johnston diagnosed her as having adjustment disorder, post-traumatic stress disorder (on account of the armed robbery in 1999) and borderline personality disorder, the symptoms being ambivalence and impulsivity. He decided she was not at high risk of killing herself or harming others.

If anything bad were to occur because of something she did, he thought this would occur not deliberately but 'by misadventure or impulsive action'. This was to prove perceptive.

Kylie was not admitted to a ward. A management plan was put in place by the hospital and staff kept in touch with her. A few days later, she faxed them a sort of 'pros and cons' sheet she'd drawn up regarding a central problem in her life: the choice between Paul and Sean. This made it clear she loved Paul and hoped they would move out west together, but she was uncertain of the strength of his love for her.

She was frustrated by his request that they keep their relationship secret. In her mind, they had reached the point where she could imagine them living together in a happy new life: 'When he can't visit me I feel hurt, angry and let down . . . He used to come and visit me a lot at first. That is now not consistent.' She wanted to strengthen their relationship, 'try to impress Paul by doing certain things.'

As for Sean, she was not sexually attracted to him, and her thoughts reveal a high level of naivety and confusion. 'I told him that I am involved in an undercover case in order to see Paul,' she recorded, 'and to continue to see Paul. I can't tell Sean what the case is because it is undercover secret squirrel stuff. And naturally he got the shits and that is how this all came about. But why couldn't he just say OK that is what you are involved in fair enough and leave it at that. Why so many questions.'

It was a volatile combination of naivety, wilfulness, and frustration. Despite this, Kylie told Lynne Baker she was feeling better, and repeated this twice in the following weeks.

★

But things had got worse at home. In early February, Sean was checking their joint email account and found a message for Kylie, which he opened. It contained sexual innuendo and was from someone he hadn't heard of before, a man named Paul Wilkinson. When he asked Kylie about it, she told him this was the policeman she was working with, and that he was nothing more than a friend.

'You've got female friends,' she said. 'I'm sure you've sent them emails like that.'

'No,' Sean replied.

Kylie reacted by becoming angry again and abusing Sean for opening an email addressed to her. She began to tell him some amazing tales about Wilkinson and his police work. These conversations would occur out in the car because she was afraid their house was bugged. She said Wilkinson was in an undercover section of the police force's State Protection Group, based at Redfern. Kylie said she had met his colleagues, including a girl who had been raped at the police academy and who later killed herself.

When the Redfern Riots occurred in the middle of February 2004, Kylie devoured the media coverage and cut out articles from the newspapers, keeping them in a manila folder. One front-page photograph showed a line of police in Redfern, facing the mob with their backs to the camera. Kylie drew a circle around one of the cops and told Sean it was the fellow she was working with, Paul Wilkinson. Sean asked her how she could identify him, and she said Wilkinson had told her.

If he had, it was untrue: ACLOs were not involved in this sort of dangerous work, and in any case Wilkinson was no longer working at Redfern. But Kylie seems to have believed it, because she had the picture laminated and later showed it to some of her family.

In early March, Kylie told Sean she had been raped by Gary. He wonders now if the rape allegation might have been an attempt to drive a wedge between himself and family members who had begun to comment on Kylie's strange behaviour. Certainly it did not bring the couple any closer together.

'When I'm on the phone [to someone],' he said to her one day in a conversation she taped, 'I've told you a million times, do not speak at all, and do not say, "Sean, Sean, Sean."'

'Sean!' she said. 'I wanted you for something. Shit. Fuck me dead!'

'I'm sick of tellin' you: we do not speak [to each other] when we're on the phone.'

'You fuckin' speak to *me* when I'm on the phone!' she said.

'Not unless I'm meant to.'

'Now what type of fucked-up thing's that?'

'Well, maybe that's the way it goes,' he said.

'Well obviously, obviously your method of speaking has failed miserably because every time we do it we fight.'

Kylie said she was worried about what Sean would say when he got into the witness box if Gary went on trial for rape. 'I've stood behind you 100 per cent,' said Sean. 'End of the day, if [Gary] did this to you, he should pay for it.'

But it turned out that what Kylie was really concerned about was whether Sean would mention Paul Wilkinson. We now know—although, of course, Sean didn't at the time—that this was due to Wilkinson's insistence that their relationship remain completely secret—he didn't want Julie finding out what he'd been up to. But Kylie told Sean the reason for the secrecy was Wilkinson's involvement in undercover activities, and so Sean agreed to keep him out of it if the matter ever went to court.

'We're going along that track [of keeping quiet about Wilkinson] because of the bullshit you're involved in,' he said. 'So, yeah, I'm gunna do it because I want to support you, but no, I do not agree with it and I never will. Because it's wrong. Simply that.'

They changed the subject and Sean mentioned the stress he was experiencing over the rape matter and other things. Kylie said she was under a lot of stress too, and Sean sounded sceptical. 'You don't even work,' he said.

She said she was on sick leave: 'I sit at home, that's what I do now . . . You think they're not hounding me to come back to find out what I'm doing? You think that, you know, it's all clear sailing? That's not pressure?'

'You don't work.'

Kylie became almost incoherent. 'I don't have that closing pressure,' she said, 'but what I have had when I was working in a clinical setting? But I still have the mental stability of the, of the pressure being outside of the setting. Right? . . . I still have to face the fact that I have to go back there one day. I have to deal with all that shit that I've had to deal with when I was there . . . Uni pressure, I've got the work pressure, I've got the home environment pressure, I've got the Coast pressure.'

'Mmm.'

'No matter what environment I walk into, I carry one

pressure load onto another. Right? . . . I'm bloody sick of this shit.'

'Yeah? Welcome to my world.'

'Oh, your world? Oh, you ought to sit in mine sometime.'

Sean accepted an awful lot of bad treatment from Kylie. 'At the time I believed what she said,' he later recalled, 'but now I just don't know. Things just don't add up.' His frustration back then was mixed with sympathy for her clearly disturbed state. Sometimes she would go to Cronulla Beach by herself and sit on the rocks and look out at the sea. On other days she'd drive over to Sydney Airport and just watch the planes come and go.

Finally, Kylie agreed to Sean's demands that they have a serious talk about their marriage. She said she wanted to ask along a friend as a mediator. Sean said this was okay, and at the appointed time a casually dressed Aboriginal man in his early thirties turned up at their place. He was of stocky build, in his early thirties, with short dark hair, about 165 centimetres tall and with a bit of a pot belly, wearing a Rabbitohs football jumper, cargo shorts and runners. He seemed to Sean to be a pleasant enough bloke, and the three of them went out onto the back patio. Sean began to ask Kylie various questions. She responded angrily, jumping out of her chair and yelling, but the man was quite good at calming her down. But the conversation was non-conclusive and after a while the man left. Sean doesn't know who he was: he says he didn't look like the pictures of Wilkinson he saw in the press several years later. On the other hand, he did look like a picture of a guy he'd seen on Kylie's mobile phone.

If it was Wilkinson, you'd have to wonder why he'd have

wanted to meet Sean in this manner. One reason might be a desire to experience some sort of thrill in deceiving his lover's husband in this way. Or there's the possibility he actually wanted Kylie out of his life: the relationship had become too intense, he feared his marriage was threatened and this was a way of ensuring Kylie talked to Sean about their problems. Whatever the case, and whoever the man was, this meeting was one of the most perplexing incidents in a story full of them.

Throughout March, Kylie was receiving phone calls and text messages almost all the time, sometimes nonstop for several hours. She would leave the house, telling Sean she was working with the undercover police. She said she was doing surveillance work in cars in the Sutherland and Menai areas, or taking photographs in Bondi. It got to the point where she insisted, before Sean took their car out, that she made a phone call first: she needed to 'clear it' with someone in the police.

One night at 3.00 a.m. she received a phone call and told Sean that 'Paul and another guy have been jumped and both beaten [during a police operation]. One has a cut to his head and one has a cut lip, they were talking to someone and someone came out of the dark and jumped them.' Kylie was in a panic, saying to the person on the phone, presumably Wilkinson, 'Are you all right? Are you all right? Just relax and stay where you are and I'll come down.'

She grabbed the first aid kit and took off, saying, 'It's only down the road—I'll be back in half an hour or so.' She came back about an hour later and there was blood on her hand and on her shirt. She told Sean she had to bandage Paul's head on the side of the road.

He asked why Wilkinson hadn't gone to hospital, and she said, 'They can't—they're not supposed to be doing what they are doing.'

Again she told him, 'They only answer to the assistant commissioner in the city.'

In mid-March, Sean went to Canberra for work and Kylie rang him, saying she urgently needed $2000. He said he didn't have that sort of money so she got her grandmother to give him a cheque, which he cashed. He asked Kylie what the money was for but she refused to say.

A week later she came to HMAS *Newcastle* and asked for another $2000, and again he asked what the money was for. Again she refused to tell him, but said, 'If I don't have it by 4.00 p.m. today, I can't guarantee my safety.'

Later that day she told him she had increased her credit card limits and taken out a personal loan. Whenever he asked her about the money after this, they would fight. Kylie's phone was keeping him awake because now it rang all night, and on 16 March they moved into separate bedrooms.

We have little idea what Kylie's life away from Sean was like in these last frenzied months, because Paul Wilkinson has never said. It must have involved constant frantic drives to meet with him, those meetings eagerly expected and often bitterly disappointing, as he refused to give her the commitment she sought and asked for yet more money to prove her love for him. She was hooked on that love, and so she raced off in shameless efforts to raise money from her husband and her family to give to the man with whom she was having an affair. Presumably, the $24,000 she borrowed at this time all went to Wilkinson.

This activity involved constant journeys through the suburbs of southern Sydney, as her life turned increasingly feral while the lives of those around her—her family, Sean, her colleagues—went on as before. By accepting Wilkinson's bait she had passed over into a darker world, and yet it was one that existed in the same physical locations as theirs, shared the same freeways and hospitals and houses and shopping centres. But now this once familiar landscape was full of her lover's assignations and crazed fantasies about persecution and undercover work, and a fictitious future together. As Kylie drove through the streets of Sydney, her mind aflame with such thoughts, other women pushed prams, and little girls—girls like she had once been—played in the front yards of the brick and tile houses. But she was no longer part of that world.

One morning Sean came home from a night shift and had a shower. He went to bed but was woken by a call from Kylie's grandmother Louisa, saying Kylie wanted him to check his phone.

He listened to a message from her: 'Read the note beside my bed. Sorry, but I had to go.' He raced up to her room and found she wasn't there. Next to the bed was a note that read: 'Life's got too hard, sorry for what I'm doing, but I have to go. Tell everyone I love them.'

Sean thought it was a suicide note and called Miranda Police Station, and two officers came around. While they were in the lounge room, Kylie came home. When she saw the police she ran outside and tried to drive off, but they stopped her and had a chat. Eventually they went away, and Kylie told Sean she wasn't going to kill herself yet, but she was close.

Kylie's anger slackened towards the end of March, but it was replaced by increased anxiety and nervousness. She was jumping at shadows and started talking about their phone and car being bugged. Whenever Sean took the car out, she still insisted on making a phone call to her police contact to 'clear it' beforehand. She told Sean she couldn't guarantee his safety if he didn't let her do this. Sean felt unnerved, and the stress built up week by week. It got to the point where she would insist not just on going out to the car but taking it for a drive in order to talk. They would pull over and chat by the side of the road. None of it made much sense to Sean. He was frightened by the fact that it seemed to make sense to Kylie.

Finally, he told her he could no longer go on as they were. The constant arguments were grinding him down: he was unhappy and losing weight, as was she. He couldn't eat or sleep normally and his health was suffering. He told her that unless she told him what was going on, they would have to go their own ways. She said she couldn't tell him what he wanted to know, that she was involved in something bigger than their arguments. He said the marriage was over and they arranged to separate.

On 23 March Kylie drove down to Kiama, on the south coast of New South Wales, for the funeral of an uncle. Carol and other members of the family were at a coffee shop when she arrived. She was sobbing uncontrollably when she got out of her car, and her mother asked what was the matter. 'Sean and I have separated,' she said. 'He's filed divorce papers.'

'You can't file them for twelve months,' said Carol. 'You can work this out.'

'We can't work it out,' said Kylie. Carol hugged her and then Kylie declared to the family, 'I'm going to say this once and only once: Sean and I are getting a divorce.' Her family were shocked by her appearance: her face was pale and pimply and she'd lost a lot of weight. And she was smoking. She told her mother for the first time about being raped by Gary, and a distressed Carol asked if she'd reported it to the police. Kylie said she had. She announced she was applying for a loan from a bank so she could have a holiday, and also that she had decided to become a police officer and had been accepted into the academy. It was a day of big announcements.

On the day the removalists arrived at Sylvania to take away Kylie's furniture, in the first week of April, she was in the best mood she'd been in for months, and Sean and she divided up their possessions amicably. He drove her to her grandmother's house for the last time, up the freeway and over the Mooney Mooney Bridge, and when they reached Erina he gave her a hug and a kiss in the driveway. Kylie shed a few tears and said she was sorry they hadn't been able to make a go of it. Sean drove off and never saw her again.

One day not long after, Kylie drove down to Sylvania to collect some small items that were still in the townhouse, and she took Louisa along. When they arrived she wouldn't let her grandmother out of the car until she'd been in and checked out the house. According to Louisa, Kylie was petrified.

Maybe she believed some of the stories Wilkinson had spun her—or maybe she was just a good actress.

Leanne thought Kylie was depressed; her face looked drawn. Often Kylie would call her at night, and she would drive down to Erina with the girls in the back of the car, pick up Kylie and take her back to her own home in Ettalong. Then Kylie would head off in Leanne's car, bringing it back in the morning when Leanne needed it for work. Kylie didn't say where she went, but later Leanne would learn that Paul Wilkinson's parents had a holiday house nearby.

After only a few visits to the Lindfield campus of her university, Kylie dropped out. When at Louisa's, she was very quiet and spent much of her time listening to the radio, writing lists and sending and receiving text messages. She was still thin but her skin cleared up and she began to eat properly. A few times a day she would go for a walk to Erina Fair, the local mall. She went to a birthday party for Leanne's two girls and there was a new spa. Everyone was using it and Kylie joined them—but she brought her phone with her.

On 13 April Kylie visited a local medical centre and learned she was pregnant. This was hugely important for two reasons, because she'd always wanted a child and because the father was Paul. There was a flurry of phone activity that day: Kylie sent 119 text messages to Paul and received ninety-one. The news must have cheered her considerably, but you have to wonder how he took it. Not all that long ago, Kylie had been complaining about not seeing him enough and questioning the strength of his love for her. It's likely the pregnancy would have increased her pressure on him to leave his family. Where previously he might have argued that his obligations to Bradley were keeping him with Julie, now that Kylie was going to have his child, she had a much stronger case.

Two days later, Kylie rang her mother and invited her to a dinner for the whole family on 22 April.

'I've decided what I'm going to do with my life,' she said, 'and I'm going to make a formal announcement.'

She also invited Leanne and her daughters, and there was a lot of talk between Louisa, Carol and Leanne about what the big announcement might be. Leanne knew that with Kylie it could be anything: she might be pregnant, or going overseas, or she might have a new boyfriend. She didn't try to get the secret from her before the dinner, knowing from experience that this would be futile.

On 20 April Kylie called Sean and sounded sad. She was crying, he recalls, and saying she still loved him, and he suggested she see someone to talk through her problems.

They had a reasonable sort of conversation, and Kylie said, 'I'm sorry. I'll make it right for you.'

Then she hung up. It's possible that this conversation indicates Wilkinson had not received the news of her pregnancy as enthusiastically as she had hoped.

The day before the big dinner, Carol rang Louisa and discussed the forthcoming announcement. Carol said she thought it would turn out to be nothing, because Kylie was a drama queen.

A few minutes after the call, Kylie rang Carol and said, 'So I'm nothing but a drama queen? You'll never know what the announcement will be, because I'm cancelling the dinner.'

In fact, the dinner went ahead, although without Carol. Beforehand, Kylie said to Louisa, 'I'll let you know in half an hour whether anyone else is turning up.' Louisa got the impression Kylie was referring to someone she hadn't met before. In half an hour, Kylie received a text message and told her grandmother, 'The person won't be coming.'

There was no big announcement at the dinner. Afterwards, when Leanne and her family had left, Kylie told Louisa she would be starting at the Police Academy on 15 May. Louisa thought she was very happy, because she'd always loved anything involving a uniform and authority. The next morning Kylie changed her story and told Louisa she was pregnant; this was the first time she'd told anyone in her family. It meant she would not be going to the academy.

'Who's the father?' said Louisa, thinking about the rape allegation. 'Is it Gary?'

'No way,' said Kylie. 'I can't tell you—you'll know as soon as I'm able to let you know.' Even now, apparently, Wilkinson was still insisting on her silence. Kylie swore Louisa to secrecy about the pregnancy. A few days later, on Monday 26 April, she drove down to Sydney to see the Rabbitohs play the Bulldogs at the Sydney Football Stadium. When she came home, Louisa saw she was upset about something but didn't find out what.

On the same day, Kylie called Sean again and had a conversation. He asked how she was going. 'Not too bad,' she said.

'Is everything sorted out?' he asked.

'Not really, but I'm getting there.' She started to cry and he said, 'Look, speak to your family. You need to speak to someone. Whatever you're involved in, you need to speak to someone about it.'

'Yes I will.'

'If you need anything, just give me a call.' She was crying a lot by now and said, 'I should do that.' It was the last time they spoke to each other.

On 28 April, Leanne drove Carol to Louisa's place in the morning, so she could borrow some money. Leanne went into Kylie's room and found her sitting on the bed, her bags already packed. Leanne had been told she was off that day to Goulburn to join the police; as instructed, Louisa had not told anyone about the pregnancy. They had a brief conversation and Leanne thought Kylie was happier than she'd been in the past few weeks. 'What time are you leaving?' she said.

'6.00 p.m.'

It was 9.00 a.m. 'Gosh,' said Leanne. 'You've got ages to wait. What are you doing?'

'Watching the minutes tick over,' said Kylie.

Leanne said goodbye. She never saw her sister again.

THE DETECTIVE

During the early months of 2005, the police investigation remained inactive; the first anniversary of Kylie's disappearance came and went. John Edwards' fears that the police had engaged in some sort of cover-up increased with another family tragedy. In February his niece, a young mother named Cassandra Girkin, also went missing. She was shopping with her husband at the Westfield mall at Tuggerah when she went to the toilets and didn't come back.

The last sight of her was on one of the mall's security cameras as she left the centre alone. It seemed to John, in his misery and confusion, too much of a coincidence that two members of his family should have disappeared from the Coast in the space of one year, and he wondered if they could be linked. (Cassandra's skeleton was found six months later, in bushland just a few hundred metres from the mall. It is not known how she died.)

John's belief in some sort of police conspiracy festered, to the point where he came to believe they made two attempts to kill him in 2005 in order to stop his investigation. The first was on the F3, as he was on his way from Sydney to Gosford Police Station to talk to detectives. A female driver came up alongside him and looked across, then swerved in front of his vehicle, almost forcing him off the road. Later he saw the woman at the police station but said nothing. The second incident was on the M4 motorway in Sydney, when a male driver tried to do the same thing. After that, John stopped his investigation. His anger and frustration remained but he was scared for the safety of himself and his family. He put copies of all the information he'd gathered onto CDs and sent them to six people around Australia he trusted, some of them ex-army colleagues. In an accompanying letter, he directed that if anything happened to him, they were to send the information to the New South Wales police commissioner.

By mid-2005, Carol and John were both depressed and hopeless with grief, and Paul Wilkinson appeared to have got away with murder.

The Police Integrity Commission is a state government agency independent of the NSW Police Force; it is charged with dealing with police misconduct. Its officers come from other states, to ensure they have no links with local police. Senior Investigators Simon Sproule and Kieran Murphy were on duty when Paul Wilkinson arrived at the commission's offices in Elizabeth Street, Sydney, on 29 June 2005, fourteen months after Kylie's disappearance, and declared he wanted to tell them about some very serious police misconduct.

Wilkinson no longer worked for the police force: he'd walked off the job in February 2004, and had finally been sacked just two weeks before coming to the PIC. He was accompanied by his parents and a journalist from the Australian Broadcasting Corporation. It was explained that these people could not be present at the interview, and after they left it began, at 10.50 a.m. The PIC hears some wild stories, but this was to be one of the most outlandish. It was also to reactivate the investigation into Kylie's disappearance.

Wilkinson told the investigators that in January 2001 the woman who later became his wife, Julie Thurecht, had been raped at knifepoint by two police officers, Geoff Lowe and Mark Paul Trevethan. Julie had been too scared to complain to the authorities, and Wilkinson had lodged a complaint with the then police minister, Michael Costa, later in 2001, after he'd started a relationship with Julie and she'd told him about the rape. 'I threw all my trust into the Police Minister's office that he was gonna put it onto the appropriate people and it was gonna be investigated thoroughly,' he said. The complaint, according to Wilkinson, had been given to the police force to investigate, and the officer responsible had improperly told Lowe and Trevethan what was going on.

From this point in the story, Trevethan (who was as innocent as Lowe) receded and Lowe became the focus of Wilkinson's anger. He claimed that in 2002 Lowe had approached him at Loftus Railway Station: 'He's pulled up, I've told him to get fucked, he's a fuckin' idiot, and he

deserves to go to jail, and if I had my way, he will go to jail.'
To which Lowe had said, 'Keep your fuckin' mouth shut or
else you're gonna end up dead.'

Wilkinson said he'd heard nothing more about his complaint to Costa's office. But in March 2005, Julie and he and
their young son, Bradley, had been in a car on the Princes
Highway when Lowe had pulled up alongside them at traffic lights, and yelled, 'Youse keep your fuckin' mouth shut!'
Wilkinson had complained to the police about this and it
had been investigated. The previous Friday, he'd received a
call from the investigating officer: 'Basically he told me I'm
full of shit and the complaint is going nowhere.' To which
Wilkinson had replied, 'Mate, I'm not happy with this at all
and I will be taking it further.'

And now he was.

Wilkinson told the PIC officers that Julie and he had separated eight months earlier. He still saw her and Bradley, and
she was reluctant for him to persist with the complaint against
Lowe. But he thought it was important because Lowe was a
major criminal.

He proceeded to tell an amazing tale of how he had been
forced to deliver bags of heroin for Geoff Lowe and Mick
Hollingsworth, the officer who'd been driving the pursuit
vehicle when TJ Hickey died. He had done this under duress:
they told him that unless he helped them, they would shoot
his wife and cut his child's throat.

If some of these stories seem vaguely familiar, it's because
they echo some of those Kylie told Sean—for example, about
rape and death threats. And now Kylie herself reappeared in
Wilkinson's fantasy world.

Wilkinson: 'They were, they were rootin' a sheila—her name's Kylie . . .'

Sproule: 'Who's Kylie . . . ?'

Wilkinson: 'She was a nurse and she was also a, worked the streets over in the Bankstown area . . . She'd been runnin' tricks with Geoff Lowe and Mick Hollingsworth . . . Yeah, she was a hooker, mate . . .'

Sproule: 'How did you meet Kylie?'

Wilkinson explained how he'd been a patient at Sutherland Hospital, where Kylie had worked: 'I'd go out the back . . . started to smoke. She came out and asked certain questions . . . Asked if I knew Geoff Lowe . . . The next day I was sneakin' another smoke [and Kylie asked,] "Your wife wouldn't happen to be Julie, would it?"

"No. Why?"

'"Did you make a complaint about rape?"

'"No. Why?" and I got warnings from her: "Keep your fuckin' mouth shut." '

It was after this, Wilkinson said, that the two policemen had forced him to deliver drugs for them, paying him for the work. The investigators asked why Lowe and Hollingsworth would have involved him in their drug-dealing. He suggested they'd wanted to implicate him in illegal activity so they'd have a hold over him. Kylie had been involved too.

Sproule: 'I'm a little confused.'

Murphy: 'I think we've missed a bit. We initially started, you said about delivering the drugs for Lowe and everybody else. You started to tell us about Kylie. I think we might have gone down the Kylie track, but we wanted to know about the drugs . . .'

Wilkinson: 'She's involved in the drugs . . .'

Murphy: 'Right.'

It wasn't right at all, of course; it was incredibly confusing. And there was more. Wilkinson went on to explain how Kylie, at one point in this increasingly incoherent story, had threatened him with a Glock pistol. At another, she had told him that Mick Hollingsworth had admitted to her he'd deliberately rammed TJ Hickey's bike. But finally, he said, the drug drops had stopped, in late April of 2004.

Murphy: 'Why did it stop?'

Wilkinson: 'Because Kylie went missing.'

Murphy: 'Okay.'

Sproule: 'She went missing. Is she still missing?'

Wilkinson: 'Yep.'

Sproule asked if Wilkinson knew where she was, and Wilkinson almost boasted about the fact that the Gosford detectives had spoken to him and examined his car. He said he used to work with Detective Rebekkah Craig at Redfern. But he offered no further information about Kylie's death and the conversation moved on.

Then, later in the interview, he casually dropped in, 'Mate, Kylie is still missing, yes. She's actually dead.'

Sproule: 'Sorry?'

Wilkinson: 'She's dead.'

Sproule: 'Oh, is she?'

Murphy: 'Do you want to tell us the story? How do you know that?'

Wilkinson had a good answer: 'Because I was there when it happened.'

He proceeded to tell the astonished investigators a story

horrific in its details, and made more so by the elaborate casualness with which he set them out. He'd been at his parents' house at Yarrawarrah in April 2004 when Geoff Lowe arrived and forced him at gunpoint to get into his utility. They drove to the nearby Royal National Park, where Lowe stopped and put a blindfold on Wilkinson. Then he drove for twenty-five minutes into the park and stopped again, telling Wilkinson to get out.

Then 'he pulled Kylie from the back of his car . . . She was bound, and he cut her toes and fingers off and stabbed her, raped her, while she was still alive, and placed her fingers and toes in a bag. I remember trying not, trying not to look, but told I had to, I actually had to go and look at her. She was trying to scream but couldn't. She had—I guess it was fuel, I don't know, don't know what it was—put on her head. He's lit it and she's lost her head . . . He cut her throat and he stabbed her several times.'

A grave had already been dug, he explained, and after removing Kylie's teeth with pliers and cutting off her head, Lowe had made Wilkinson bury her body. The head was buried nearby.

Lowe then put the blindfold back on Wilkinson and drove him to the entrance of the park, where he left him, telling him that if he told anyone what he'd seen, his son would be next.

Murphy said, 'Why would he want to murder her? Do you know that?'

Wilkinson: 'She wanted to break away from it, from all the shit that's gone on, you know, the drug trade. She wanted to break away from all of that.'

When they'd finished with the details, Kieran Murphy said, 'Paul, we started today and we went through a number of matters and concerns of yours and allegations. Why didn't you bring up the murder when we first started our conversation?'

It was a good question. Wilkinson had seemed more interested in talking about his wife being raped by Geoff Lowe than about Kylie's horrific death.

Wilkinson: 'I'll be honest with you, I really didn't know whether I could trust coming to the PIC either, but after speaking to you blokes, I knew that youse weren't here to piss in me pocket.'

Later, Murphy said, 'You understand, obviously you understand, you know, murder is a very serious allegation. Why haven't you reported it to any other police?'

Wilkinson: 'Well, I'm not gonna have my son go, be the next person.'

Murphy: 'Right. Okay, so what's changed your mind now?'

Wilkinson: 'Fuck, it's gotta stop.'

Murphy: 'Right.'

Wilkinson: 'It's gotta stop. I'm sick and tired of this prick comin' around my fuckin' house, toying with me.'

He'd told them Geoff Lowe had been visiting his home and threatening him. He now added a story about a time he'd been seized by police one night outside the Engadine RSL after some trouble with the bouncers. He said the senior police officer present was about to take him home when Geoff Lowe had turned up, and 'next minute I'm in the back of a fuckin' paddy wagon, gettin' me head, you know, punched in the head.'

★

The PIC officers were deeply sceptical about what they were hearing, but they were obliged to check it out. The first step was to take Wilkinson seriously as he sat in the room there with them, to ask him for details which they were almost certain were being invented. This was how the law enforcement and justice systems were to respond to Wilkinson again and again over the next few years, by treating his ravings with a respect we now know they did not deserve. If anyone had seen the whole pattern of the man, they might have stopped and decided to go no further. But everyone saw only a piece of the pattern, and that piece had to be dealt with by the rules. They weren't bad rules, but the people who wrote them hadn't been thinking of someone like Paul Wilkinson.

'All right,' said Murphy, 'don't take this the wrong way, but I'm just telling you, there can be serious repercussions if a lot of time and money is spent investigating these serious matters and they come to nothing. You understand that people who give out information can be in a lot of trouble themselves then, you understand?'

Wilkinson had no problem with this. 'Well,' he said, 'it's not my fault if things can't be found.'

Murphy agreed, but stressed again how serious it would be if the allegations turned out to be a waste of time. Wilkinson assured them he wasn't there 'to piss in your pocket'.

After two hours the interview concluded and the investigators made a copy of a nine-page written statement that Wilkinson had brought with him, summarising his allegations. They arranged for him to accompany them to the Royal National Park the next day and show them Kylie's graves.

Late that afternoon, Wilkinson called to say his family

had advised he have a legal representative with him during the visit to the park. He promised to let Sproule know the next morning if he had been able to arrange a lawyer. The next day a solicitor named Frances McGowan called the PIC to say she was acting for Wilkinson, and would be unable to come with them to the national park for two weeks because of a court matter she was involved in. Sproule explained how important the search was but McGowan said she could do nothing for a fortnight.

On 11 July Sproule called Wilkinson to follow up on some matters raised in the interview, and Wilkinson was edgy. He asked why they needed to know more, and Sproule reminded him that at the end of the interview they'd told him they'd need to talk again, and he'd agreed. Wilkinson said he'd get his 'legal people' to deal with it. On 15 July McGowan called Sproule to say any visit to the national park would be further delayed because there was to be a conference next week between Wilkinson, herself and a barrister named Terry Healey.

This was the beginning of a series of delays involving different people that was to stretch out Wilkinson's dealings with investigators and the justice system for four more years. The causes of these delays included the number and complexity of his lies, his frequent changes of mind and the slow-moving nature of the legal world. These delays were to increase the already heavy burden of grief on Kylie's family, who still knew almost nothing about the course of the investigation or Paul Wilkinson.

Nothing more happened in July, and on 3 August Terry Healey called Simon Sproule and announced that he had been instructed by Wilkinson to say where Kylie's body was. In fact, they had someone at the location at that moment, a forensic consultant named Carl Hughes. Fifteen minutes later, Sproule and Kieran Murphy set off for the Royal National Park. Sproule had been in touch with Andrew Waterman at the Homicide Squad and now rang him with the good news. Waterman said he'd wait to see what they found before he sent anyone out. The number of police involved in searches for graves can be considerable, and he wanted to make sure there was good cause to commit resources.

At 5.50 p.m. the investigators met Carl Hughes on the Gundamaian fire trail in the Royal National Park, and Hughes told them this was the third time in a fortnight he'd been out with Wilkinson looking for the grave. Wilkinson believed he'd found it today and had left after identifying the place. It was off the trail near a large gum tree, and the ground appeared to have been slightly turned over. By the time Sproule and Murphy had examined the site it was growing dark. Sproule called Andrew Waterman, who said he'd send some people out the next day. He arranged for uniformed police from Sutherland to guard the site overnight.

At 9.50 a.m. the next morning the PIC investigators met in the national park with quite a crowd. It included Carl Hughes, forensic officers, more police from Sutherland and the Homicide Squad, and others including a botanist from the National Parks and Wildlife Service, which managed the park. Rebekkah Craig had been told the search was to occur but was advised not to attend, to her disappointment. Wilkinson himself was not there.

Hughes walked them to the possible grave site, the

proceedings being carefully filmed by a police photographer. A cadaver dog went over the area, without finding anything. Then the digging began. The search occupied most of the day but nothing was found. The digging revealed extensive and intact tree root systems just below the surface, which the botanist said were well over two years old, indicating the ground hadn't been dug for at least that long. Kylie had disappeared only fifteen months before. When Carl Hughes was told this, he indicated a new area nearby, which was also dug up without result. At 5.15 p.m. the search was abandoned.

The cost and effort had been considerable. The search involved, apart from the PIC officers, five detectives from Sutherland, four Homicide investigators, four Crime Scene staff, two National Parks staff, four Crime Scene guards and one cadaver dog ($100 an hour for three hours). The total cost was $20,804.

The PIC and Homicide officers were, naturally, concerned by the failure to find a grave. Sproule tried to contact Wilkinson but he didn't ring back. On 13 December Sproule called again and the phone was answered by a male who claimed to be Wilkinson's brother, although Sproule thought it was Wilkinson himself. The man said Wilkinson was unhappy with what the PIC had done but declined to say why. The next day Sproule called the number again and had a conversation with Wilkinson's mother, asking that Paul contact him urgently. He never heard from Wilkinson again.

If Paul Wilkinson had not walked into the PIC's offices that July, he would almost certainly be a free man today. But the allegations he made were so serious that they had to be investigated, and so it was that Strike Force Bergin was reactivated. Detective Peter Houlahan had moved on, so the bosses at Gosford looked around for someone else to lead the investigation. Some of the senior detectives wanted no part in the job: the prospect of spending months investigating Wilkinson's crazy stories was of no appeal at all. Eventually, the bosses' eyes settled on a thirty-two-year-old detective who had transferred from the Homicide Squad earlier that year.

Glenn Smith grew up in western Sydney and had wanted to be a cop ever since he was a kid, inspired by television programs like *Chips* and *Starsky and Hutch*. But he didn't like the authority structure of school and left at the end of Year Ten, aged fifteen. To be a police officer you have to complete Year Twelve.

Smith became a graphic designer, working with a legal publisher. By the time he reached his early twenties, the predictability and the indoor life got to him and he started to feel the tug of his old ambition. He completed his Higher School Certificate at night and entered the Police Academy at the age of twenty-two. He became a cop and enjoyed it, liking the variety of work and moving from uniform to detectives after assisting in a few murder investigations when he was stationed at Glebe. He married, and when his wife became pregnant they decided they had to buy a house. They could afford the outer western suburbs or the Central Coast, which for them meant there was no choice: they moved up to a suburb near Brisbane Waters, and Glenn Smith, like thousands of others, began the daily commute down the F3 and over the Mooney Mooney Bridge.

He didn't plan to end up in Homicide, knowing it would disrupt his home life with its long and unpredictable hours. These days, most police work involves regular work rhythms, but the Homicide Squad is different. Its unofficial slogan is 'Our day begins when yours ends'. When its detectives are on call, they can find themselves anywhere in the state at a few hours' notice. Investigations can involve very long hours in the first week, and can sometimes take them away from home for a month or more. But despite this, the squad was where Smith's experience led him—in his early work as a general detective he continued to get involved with murders and he made plenty of contacts in Homicide. One day he was asked to join, and he was fortunate over the next few years to work with some of the state's best homicide investigators, such as Andrew Waterman and Paul Jacob.

Once Smith's second child was born, the Homicide hours became just too much and he transferred to Brisbane Waters Detectives to be near home. His wife needed him. Two weeks after he arrived in Gosford, he was working on a Sunday when he got his first murder as OIC (officer in charge). The case was pretty remarkable: a man named Paul Renete had killed a friend's mother and then slashed his own wrists and mutilated his penis, before jumping on his pushbike and riding down to the end of the street, where he fell off and was found. It was a so-called 'smoking gun' case: Renete admitted his responsibility. There was no trial and he was found not guilty according to the McNaughton Rules, meaning he was insane. He ended up in a mental institution.

Smith had just wrapped up that investigation when he was called into the office of his crime manager and told that

Strike Force Bergin was to recommence and he was to be the OIC. Smith knew about the case. While working in Homicide, he had come up with Andrew Waterman twice when the inspector was advising Craig on the investigation. When he'd transferred to Gosford he'd read through the documentation: it was an interesting 'whodunit' but also something of a poisoned chalice because it had been dragging on so long, with no sign of an arrest in sight. At one stage Gosford had actually tried to pass it over to Homicide, which had declined the offer.

But Paul Wilkinson was a challenge, and Smith liked a challenge. It was August 2005, sixteen months since Kylie had disappeared. He began by reading all the documentation again and discussing it with Rebekkah Craig, who was still on the investigation, and Andrew Waterman. He came up with a plan of attack and realised he would have trouble getting time to work the investigation from the Gosford office, because Craig and he would be expected to help with the other cases that kept pouring in. So he persuaded the bosses to let Bergin operate out of the Homicide Squad office for a while.

He returned to Parramatta and found himself one desk away from where he'd been working not so long ago. Some of Waterman's team assisted when they could, and Smith was also given two junior officers from Sutherland, although he lost one when the man announced that he knew Geoff Lowe. The remaining one was a plainclothes constable, Ben Mang, a young man with a pleasantly dry sense of humour.

The detectives paid a lot of attention to the nature of Wilkinson's lies, of which they now had many examples, wondering if they meant anything at all. They needed to understand them if they were to understand Paul Wilkinson, but it was not easy. Usually criminals lie to cover their tracks, but while some of Wilkinson's stories fell into this category, others didn't. Many were bizarre fantasies that had served only to draw attention to him. Maybe there were elements of truth mixed up with his lies—but which were which?

A great deal of time over the next few months was spent investigating what Wilkinson had told the PIC and disproving it, step by step. Despite the implausibility of his allegations, this had to be done, because Smith was trying to build a circumstantial case that Wilkinson had killed Kylie. This involved ruling out any alternative explanation for her death that might be brought up by the defence during a trial.

Smith wanted desperately to find Kylie's body, for the sake of proving she was dead, for the sake of her family and also for any forensic evidence it might provide. He sometimes thought of the family, of their need for a grave where they could go and grieve. Without a body, they would always wonder where Kylie was. Maybe lying in the bush somewhere? Or at the bottom of some river?

John Edwards' first reaction on meeting Glenn Smith was disappointment. The detective looked even younger than his years, and with his gelled blond hair and easy manner, he was not the senior figure John believed was needed to uncover the truth about his daughter's disappearance. He felt let down. 'This is a whitewash,' he said to himself. 'They've thrown all of this onto this young guy and it's just not going to happen.'

But this soon changed. Smith realised there'd been a breakdown in relations between the police and the family, and tried to get some order back into things by saying that from now on communication would be regular but controlled: only one detective would talk to one member of the family, once a week. He said the person he'd speak to would be John.

Carol wasn't happy with that and rang the Gosford superintendent, who insisted the detectives talk to her as well. So Smith talked to John, and Craig talked to Carol, on a weekly basis. (Later this dropped back to fortnightly, and when Craig went on maternity leave, Smith talked to Carol too.) This regular contact meant a great deal to the Edwards. It was something John says had never happened before. From the police point of view, that is perhaps understandable: it must be very hard to call the father of a woman who has almost certainly been murdered and to have to tell him, week after week for months, that no progress has been made. But for John, hearing nothing had been even worse than hearing bad news. Now at least he knew that the police were still working on Kylie's disappearance, that someone in authority cared.

And it wasn't all bad news. Some weeks, Smith would say to John, 'We've got some lines of inquiry going. I can't tell you anything about it but we're still moving. It's slow, and I'm sorry about that.' But at least there was movement.

Smith and Craig were becoming familiar with some of Wilkinson's obsessions. They'd read the transcript of his PIC interview and learned that one part of it was true: he had lodged a complaint with police alleging Geoff Lowe had threatened him while stopped at traffic lights. That complaint had been rejected not long after Wilkinson was sacked by the police force, and his anger at these events had probably driven him to approach the PIC. The detectives learned that his wife, Julie, had been in the car with him at the lights and had refused to support his version of events. Now they wondered if they should have a word with her too. Houlahan and Craig had never tried to talk to her, figuring she would side with Paul. But now she had separated from Wilkinson, and maybe the time had come to chat.

On 4 November 2005 Smith and Craig obtained permission to place a telephone intercept on Wilkinson's mobile. For many months Ben Mang spent long hours wearing headphones in a small room, listening to Wilkinson's rambling phone conversations. The work was mind-numbing at times: Mang had to write a summary of every call, as well as reading all of Wilkinson's text messages and noting any of interest. Many of these calls and text messages were made to a female friend in Victoria named Cheryl Kaulfuss. There was a large number of them: Wilkinson was unemployed and seemed to live through his phone. In the first two months, police monitored over 2500 outgoing and incoming texts and calls. Some of these became part of the Crown's case and so can be quoted here.

On 11 November 2005 he texted a female contact: 'Received letter from Internal affairs they DON'T believe my story RE murder of that girl.' On 16 November he texted Cheryl Kaulfuss: 'Im FUMIN, these bastards hav gone 2 a all time low. They followed my mother and she honestly thought she was goin 2 join that girl in the Royal National Park.'

Later that night he spoke with Kaulfuss and said, 'The barrister refuses to do anything without the body, and I said [to him], "Well, you're not getting one, because I haven't got any insurance." ' On 4 December he told his cousin Brigette Fernando that the detectives should be looking at other police for Kylie's murder, and then he texted Julie Thurecht: 'Well there u hav it im GOIN DOWN 4 A CRIME THAT CUNT COMMITTED and u still sittin at home letting RAPIST MURDERING CUNTS GET AWAR WITH IT.'

There it was again, a recurrence of Wilkinson's obsession with the idea that his wife had been raped by Geoff Lowe. Smith decided to talk with Lowe, who was still a police officer. But first he would see if Julie Thurecht would agree to an interview.

THE WIFE

Julie Thurecht was an only child and had a typical upbringing in the Sutherland Shire. Sydney's southernmost coastal area is blessed with rich vegetation growing on ridges between attractive and often deep valleys, some containing creeks and rivers. It's bounded by Cronulla Beach and the Royal National Park to the east, and the big Georges River to the north. The buildings in the Shire (as it is fondly known) are mainly houses, running along the ridges and spilling halfway down the valleys, thanks to the firm foundations provided by the Hawkesbury sandstone, which breaks the soil everywhere among the plentiful trees and bushes.

Almost the only institutions to be seen as you travel through the leafy suburbs are schools, of which there are many, and ovals. The area is fairly Anglo—the Cronulla Riots of January 2006 were caused by disputes with Lebanese youths from other parts of Sydney. The Shire lacks extremes of wealth and poverty, and many of its residents, who tend to be passionate about the area, are tradesmen and white-collar workers. It's a traditional Australian suburban idyll, and as you wander its empty streets on a warm weekday, it's hard to imagine anything really bad happening there.

Julie's parents' brick-and-tile house in Illawong sits on one of the Shire's many streets jutting into bushland, on the side of a valley so steep that there are no houses across the road. The garden and house are meticulously maintained, the walls of the lounge room covered in old photos of bike races: Julie's father, Kevin, was once a racing cyclist. He later became a bank manager, and her mother, Jenene, ran a dry-cleaning business.

Julie has always been close to her parents. As an energetic and cheerful child she had lots of friends. She went to Menai High School and then to business school, after which she worked as a medical receptionist. Her life was like that of thousands of young women, but in early 2001 she did something ordinary that, thanks to some unfortunate twists of fate, was to have some extraordinary consequences: she had a very brief fling with a policeman named Geoff Lowe.

Soon after, she started to train to be a police officer herself. She'd always wanted to be a cop but her father hadn't supported her, not wanting his daughter to spend her working life dealing with criminals. But once she turned twenty-one, she applied to join the police and was accepted. She went to the academy and did a secondment at Bankstown, working twelve-hour shifts helping some people and arresting others. It was busy work, often exciting. She got on with the officers she was working with and loved the whole experience.

Julie first met Paul Wilkinson in July 2001, when he gave a lecture at the academy on his work as an Aboriginal Community Liaison Officer. Later, a mutual acquaintance introduced them in the bar. She found him funny and charming, and after that night he began sending her text messages; before long, they were seeing each other. He seemed to be an ordinary, pleasant bloke who had grown up in a southern Sydney suburb and was a mad-keen Souths supporter. They began a relationship and started living together the following May.

Paul had been born on 4 December 1975, the son of Ron, a fitter and turner, and June, an Aboriginal woman. They'd met when Ron was pig-shooting in Walgett in 1974. Paul went to Engadine High School, where he didn't do particularly well academically but was good at sport. He left at the end of Year Eleven and worked as a security guard at Garden Island before getting a job at Royal Prince Alfred Hospital. He became an ACLO in 1997.

When Julie first met him she didn't know what an ACLO was, and from the way he talked in the early period of their relationship she assumed it must be some sort of plainclothes cop. He didn't actually say this, but the way he talked about his job made it sound like that.

The Wilkinson family was different to Julie's. A lot of time was spent drinking and gambling, and June was a regular at the Sutherland United Services Club. They swore a lot. But June and Ron made Julie feel welcome, and before long she was getting along well with them. Paul was as close to his parents as she was to hers, and she began to spend a lot of time at their place, also a red-brick house on a dead-end street jutting into the bush. Yarrawarrah is in the south of the

Shire, and the Wilkinson house is a bit smaller and older than most in the street. Today the concrete driveway up the steep block is heavily cracked, with a big tin letterbox standing at the bottom with no number on it.

Julie's parents first met Paul when she brought him home for dinner. He was wearing a South Sydney football top and jeans. Like almost everyone who met him, at first they found him articulate and charming. Their one concern, as they learned more about him, was that he didn't have anything to his name, not even a car. This seemed strange for a man in his mid-twenties who'd been working for years. But Paul had an explanation: he said he'd used all his money to repay his mother's gambling debts, so his parents wouldn't lose their house.

Other than this, he didn't seem to have any vices. He liked AC/DC and country music, especially Charlie Pride. His food tastes were basic—he was just a meat-and-veg man. He smoked a lot but told Julie he was staunchly against drugs. She saw him drink only a few times: he said he'd seen what alcohol had done to some of his relatives and didn't want to turn out like that himself. His one indulgence was Coca-Cola, of which he consumed up to four litres a day.

Paul didn't push himself forward in conversation, although he had plenty to say when asked. Kevin and Jenene got the impression from what he did say that he must be an important figure at work. So did Julie. When they were at home, he would talk all the time, for hours on end, often about his achievements at Redfern. He always seemed to be the knight in shining armour. Once, for example, he told Julie how a newborn baby was being thrown around by Aboriginal people at Redfern Park; he'd gone in and rescued the child, saving the day. There were a lot of stories like that.

Around September, one of her friends let slip that Julie had slept with Geoff Lowe. Paul had shown intense jealousy when he learned of other men Julie had had sexual relationships with before she met him, but with Lowe it was far more fierce, for some reason. Over the next few months he brooded on her brief liaison with Lowe, and in time it became a fierce obsession. He asked her to change her diary and put in an entry saying she had been raped by the policeman. She refused. Then he showed her a letter he had written and was about to give to a police officer at Redfern, accusing Geoff Lowe of rape. She read it with astonishment.

'Are you going to back me up?' he said. 'Come on, back me up.'

'No, Paul. It's wrong.'

'Well, if you loved me you would.'

In October 2001, the duty officer at Redfern rang Julie to tell her that Paul had been bitten by a criminal. When he came home, he had tooth marks on his wrist. Julie had always wondered about Paul's claim that he'd been stabbed by a syringe before she met him, but she didn't have any evidence either way. Now she looked at his hand—it didn't seem too bad. But Paul made a big deal of it, which she knew by now was his nature: he liked to dramatise things. He took a year's stress leave after the incident. Julie thought he still quite liked his job, but the hours had been getting to him. He was not a morning person and had been pulling a lot of seven-to-three shifts. Now he got to sleep in every day, on full pay.

It's a fact of police life that while the work can be hard

and sometimes dangerous, the provisions for leave and even retirement if something goes wrong are relatively generous; as a result, they are often rorted.

Julie pushed on with her training but noticed Paul becoming increasingly unhappy. He started trying to talk her out of becoming a police officer, saying, 'All male coppers are sleazes.' By this time she knew what an ACLO really was and had detected that Paul resented colleagues who were police officers. This exploded on her birthday in January 2002, when Geoff Lowe sent her a joking text message with a sexual reference, which Paul saw. She tried to explain this away, but he was furious and typed up another complaint alleging that her sexual encounter with Lowe back in January 2001 had been rape, and that it had involved another police officer and been conducted at knifepoint. Julie again refused to support the complaint, but Paul put pressure on her and later she gave it to Redfern police, but did not pursue it. This set a pattern for the next few years: Wilkinson had Julie in his power but there were limits. If he tried to involve her in anything illegal she would resist, which he accepted although it made him bitter.

Finally, he told her that if she became an officer, she would have more power than him and that this would be bad for their relationship. 'If you love me,' he said, 'you'll leave the police.'

She resisted his requests she stop her training, but when she did her placement at Bankstown he made her life hell, ringing her frequently and turning up to talk with her. In the end he wore her down: she gave up and resigned. He'd forced her to choose between the job and himself, and she'd chosen

Smiley Kylie (sitting on her father's knee)
All photos courtesy of John and Carol Edwards unless otherwise indicated

Kylie in red

Kylie's wedding, 2003 (with her father)

Kylie and Sean

Paul Wilkinson and Julie Thurecht
Courtesy of Julie Thurecht

One of the searches for the grave near Mooney Mooney Creek, 2008
Courtesy of NSW Police Force

Paul Wilkinson outside Sutherland Police Station on the day he was arrested in 2007 © *Newspix/John Grainger*

Detective Constable Glenn Smith at the Supreme Court after Paul Wilkinson was sentenced in 2009 © *AAP Image/Katelyn Catanzariti*

him. She says now she doesn't know if this was because she loved him or because she'd already fallen under his control. She was ashamed to tell her parents the real reason for what she'd done. Already she was defending Paul by hiding things from them.

Paul had family at Dubbo and Walgett and talked about moving there. Julie made a few visits out west and was shocked by the way his relatives lived, the constant drunkenness and pot-smoking, the abuse and domestic violence and poor living conditions. No one seemed to have a job. The women were constantly having babies: one, a few years younger than Julie, already had five children. It was a concern to her that Paul was so attracted to this lifestyle. She came back with no desire to leave Sydney.

Despite the fact he saw his own parents frequently, Paul was jealous of Julie's close relationship with her own father and mother. He told them she was too dependent on them, and in May 2002 took her to live at Umina on the Central Coast. It seemed to Jenene that Paul felt like he was the man who ought to be in control of Julie, but so long as they were in Sydney, Kevin would keep his influence over her.

The move to Umina led to more of the financial problems Julie had come to accept as part of life with Paul. Even though he was being paid while on stress leave, he never had much money. The couple drove a car that was on permanent loan from Julie's parents. Now they used her Visa card, which was linked to her father's account, to pay the bond and furnish the new flat. The only thing Paul contributed was a television set. Things never got much better financially: Kevin paid the bond on the next two homes in which the couple lived.

In July 2002, Julie announced to her parents that Paul and she were getting married. Kevin was unhappy—he hadn't been very impressed by what he'd seen of Paul lately. For whatever reason, Wilkinson was a financial black hole. And Kevin had begun to doubt the truthfulness of some of the stories Paul told, which so often put himself in a very good light. Another problem was Paul's desire to isolate Julie from her old friends. He wanted her to be with him all the time, usually alone, sometimes with his own friends. As a result, Julie was now seeing little or nothing of people she'd known for much of her life. Kevin shared his doubts with Jenene, who'd noticed herself that Paul was a somewhat solitary character, often falling out with what friends he did have. Julie was being sucked into his narrow world, in which the main other people were his parents. Jenene and Kevin met them and found June very reserved. Ron was more open than his wife, but almost his only topic of conversation was rugby league.

Despite their concerns about the proposed marriage, Kevin and Jenene said nothing to Julie, deciding to support her in what she wanted.

Wilkinson's obsession with Geoff Lowe continued. In February 2003, a few weeks before the wedding, Julie was alone one night and received three calls from a man who did not identify himself. Each time he said, 'Keep your mouth shut or I'll kill you.' It sounded like Paul, although the voice was muffled. After the third call, she rang Paul to tell him about the calls, not asking if it had been him. He sounded upset and said he was going to contact the police. Soon, an officer from Sutherland Police Station rang Julie, saying Paul had come in and was standing next to him.

'Do you have any idea who made the calls?' said the officer. Julie told him she had no idea.

Some time later, Paul called her in a rage, and yelled, 'Why didn't you say you thought it was Geoff Lowe?'

'Lowey has no reason to threaten me,' she said. 'Was it you?'

Paul denied it for a while but finally admitted it had been him. 'It will help put more weight on the rape allegations,' he said.

Later the couple met up and Paul drove to the pay phone in Loftus where he said he'd made the call. He got out of the car and went over to the phone, which he wiped with a cloth. When he got back into the car he told her he'd been removing his fingerprints.

In retrospect, this was a turning point in Wilkinson's life, the first time we know of where he fabricated death threats, which were to become a major tool in his manipulation of the people around him and their families.

They kept coming. One day he showed Julie a piece of paper with a threatening message on it, composed of words cut out of a newspaper. It was something to do with Aboriginal deaths in police custody. Paul insisted their lives were in danger as a result of the work he'd done, and said Julie must stay at her parents' until the wedding. Julie accepted what he was saying and moved back to Illawong. This was to happen several more times over the coming year. Presumably, Wilkinson did this to get time away from Julie, although on this first occasion we do not know for what purpose.

Jenene was not as concerned about the approaching wedding as Kevin was. She felt caught between his concerns and

Julie's enthusiasm, and would be positive when she was with her daughter. Julie now says she was actually having doubts herself just before the wedding, as she became increasingly aware of Paul's controlling nature. On her hen's night, he hung around the venue and learned that she'd danced with one of the actors in the show the women had gone to see; afterwards there was an explosion of jealousy. Julie says she pushed her concerns away, thinking maybe they were just normal pre-marriage nerves. In any case, she told herself, it was too late to stop: people were coming to the wedding from overseas and interstate. Plane tickets had been booked.

In February 2003, she and Paul were married at St Andrew's Anglican Church in Cronulla. There were 130 people there, including many of Paul's colleagues from Redfern. At this stage he was still liked by most of the people he worked with, who found him easy to get on with and apparently enthusiastic about his job. The reception was held at the Novotel at Brighton-le-Sands, and lots of Paul's extended family from Dubbo and Walgett were there. This was an eye-opener for Julie's family. They were vastly outnumbered by the Wilkinson clan, who obviously enjoyed a party. Some had made an effort but others were dressed in casual clothes, as though they'd just come off the street. One, from west of the mountains, tried to steal Julie's uncle's jacket. Another, who hadn't been asked, turned up anyway and tried to punch the bride for not inviting him.

In the months after the wedding, Paul became increasingly unsociable. By the second half of 2003, he and Julie hardly saw his old friends at all—most of hers had already been driven away—and their social life had become restricted to their own home and visits to their parents every few days. This didn't worry Julie so much, because by now she was pregnant and concentrating on becoming a mother. But she did notice the isolation increased Paul's desire to control her. For a while he was even fiercely jealous of her gynaecologist.

In September 2003 they moved to the rented house in Kelvin Parade, Picnic Point, in preparation for the birth. On 18 November Julie was due to be induced and Paul dropped her at the hospital at 10.00 a.m. and sped off, telling her he was going to get new tyres for the car. Julie started pushing at 1.30 p.m. and said to the female friend who was with her, 'Could you please ring Paul and get him back in here?'

He just made it for the birth but left again an hour later. He returned briefly that evening, announcing that he had a headache and was going home to sleep. Later that night there was a crisis when Bradley stopped breathing. Julie rang Paul in a panic while the child was being resuscitated and he tore shreds off her for calling him so late. This was not like Paul, who was very much a night person, and she wondered what he was up to.

It turned out he'd celebrated his son's birth by cleaning out their joint bank account. He got paid the day Bradley was born, and when Julie left hospital and went online to their joint bank account to pay the rent, she saw that Paul had withdrawn all his wages at the Sutherland United Services Club on the night of the birth. They were all gone, gambled away. A friend lent her enough to tide them over for the next fortnight.

On leaving hospital, Julie went to her parents' for a few days so her mother could help with the child, and then wanted to move back to Picnic Point. But there was a problem. Paul said he'd received more death threats in the past few days, and for their own safety, Bradley and she should remain at her parents'. Julie agreed. Today she has no idea why he wanted to keep her away at this time, before his affair with Kylie began. Possibly he was just not looking forward to sharing the house with a newborn baby. One thing he didn't do was take refuge in work, as many men do: he was on sick leave for most of the time from November until the following February.

In December Wilkinson blacked out and went into Sutherland Hospital for a few days to have his sugar levels tested. It was hard for Julie to keep up with all his health issues by now, what with his stress and all the rest. Recently he'd told her he'd been diagnosed as having some sort of psychosis. She discussed this with her parents but they all found it hard to believe: they knew Paul was lazy and told a lot of stories, but they had no suspicion of any deeper problems. Kevin wondered if Paul had fooled the expert who'd made the diagnosis. There was no doubt his son-in-law was a good actor, and cunning too.

Julie moved back home just before Christmas, unaware that Paul had begun his affair with Kylie. She did not find out about it for many years. She was vulnerable to deception for several reasons: her acceptance of Paul's longstanding odd behaviour; her focus on her newborn child; and the amount of time she spent at her parents'.

Wilkinson picked vulnerable women and preyed on them. He made sure they were trusting by nature, because part of his technique involved portraying himself as a victim in order to gain their sympathy. Once he had their attention, he took their money—in Julie's case, also her father's—and grew bored. This still lay ahead for Kylie.

When the Redfern Riots occurred in February 2004, Paul told Julie that the police had had nothing to do with TJ Hickey's death. He'd visited Redfern and chatted with former colleagues and confirmed this, he said. The claim that Mick Hollingsworth had pursued TJ to his death was false, he told her—it was just the local Aboriginal people trying to cause trouble. But a few weeks later he changed his story: he said he'd been told Hollingsworth had killed TJ after all.

At the same time he told Julie this, the death threats started to arrive again. This time they were in what looked like female handwriting. At first Paul was hesitant about showing them to police, but on Julie's insistence he did. (Or at least, he said he did.) After receiving three threats in one week, he demanded she return to her parents'. She did for a while and then insisted on coming home again. Paul picked Bradley and her up, and when they reached home told her to wait in the car while he checked the place out. After a while he came out and said, 'I don't want you going in there—someone has been in there.'

She insisted on going inside, where she found one of Bradley's teddy bears stuck to the wall with a knife through its throat. The knife was also pinning a sheet of paper with the words 'Bye bye baby Bradley'. The portable cot had been turned upside down in the lounge room and a few other things were scattered around the house on the floor. There was also (as Wilkinson was to tell detectives a few months later) the word 'Die' written in pen on the fridge. Paul insisted that Julie and Bradley go back and stay at her parents' yet again, which they did.

In retrospect, Julie now sees that Paul wanted her out of the way so he could conduct his affair with Kylie. But at the time, she believed his story that he was being persecuted for trying to do the right thing and reveal the truth about police involvement in TJ Hickey's death. Over the next few months he would visit Julie at her parents' most days in the afternoon and remain for about half an hour. He would not normally stay for dinner, saying he had to get home to keep an eye on the house 'in case anything happened'.

Julie had little idea what else he was doing with his time. As we have seen, in February 2004 he left Marrickville Police Station and never returned to work. He told Julie he had punched a police officer but a few weeks later a senior officer called her to ask what had happened to Paul, who she said had just walked off the job one day for no apparent reason. He later told a former colleague he had cancer.

On 14 March, Kevin received his Visa card bill and it showed thousands of dollars that had been spent by Paul. He blew his top and told Julie he was sick of her moving between Picnic Point and Illawong: she had to make a choice. Julie called Paul and he drove around to take her home. Once Julie and Bradley were in the car, he came back into the house and told Julie's parents they would never see Bradley again. He made a great drama of this declaration, saying they could throw him out of their house, but not their grandchild. When he'd gone, Kevin was really upset: Jenene and he had become deeply attached to Bradley. The next day, Jenene called Julie and she came around; Kevin told her why he'd been so angry the day before and how there was no desire to exclude Bradley from their lives.

Although Kevin and Jenene were still susceptible to Wilkinson's influence, their suspicions were growing. The next day they changed their wills to make sure that if anything happened to Julie, Paul could not benefit from their deaths: the money would go into a trust for Bradley. It was not that they feared any violence from Paul, but rather a reaction to the financial problems he had introduced into their daughter's life and their own. By now they knew he was a serious problem gambler who often got into financial trouble. At one point Julie had even taken his cashcard and kept it for a while so he wouldn't gamble away all their money.

Despite this, by the end of March Paul suddenly had lots of cash—so much that in early April he took his family on a short holiday to Batemans Bay. Julie had no idea where it came from—she would learn much later that Kylie had given it to Paul—and didn't ask. By now she'd given up trying to understand his actions.

Late one night, not long after they returned from Batemans Bay, Julie dropped her mobile phone into the bath. When she pulled it out it wouldn't work, and she asked Paul if she could borrow his phone to use with another SIM card she had. When she turned it on she saw that Paul had some messages stored in his phone, so she had a look. One was from someone called 'Hutch'. She opened it and saw a picture of a horse and cart, and underneath this the words: 'I'm hurrying to see you soon, I love you.'

Julie tried to save the message to her SIM card but rang the number by mistake. When she realised what she'd done, she hung up. A few minutes later a message came through from the same number: 'Who is this and why are you ringing me at this hour.' Julie texted back, saying, 'Sorry I had the wrong number and I was looking for my friend Matt.' She pulled her SIM card out of the phone and returned it to Paul, who put his back in and went up the road to the shops. When he returned he was very angry: he walked into the bedroom and demanded, 'Who the hell is Matt?'

Julie said, 'Who the hell is that sending those kind of messages to you?'

'It's a girl called Kylie,' said Paul. 'I've been working on a sexual-assault case with her, and that was actually a message that she sent to the guy who assaulted her.'

Julie had never heard of Kylie before. They proceeded to have an argument about why he was still involved in work when he'd told her he'd left, and whether he was actually having an affair with this Kylie.

'Don't you trust me?' he said.

Julie knew that Paul had a shocking temper, and by this stage it was easier not to provoke him, so she let it go. But for the first time she suspected he was cheating on her.

On 26 April 2004 there was a Souths game, and Julie and Paul decided to go. They dropped by Illawong on the way, and just as they were about to leave, Paul persuaded Julie not to come after all. It looked like rain, and he said he was concerned Bradley might get wet. Kevin noticed Paul go into Julie's old bedroom and remove a Souths jumper, which he stuffed under the one he was already wearing. He wondered what was going on but knew there was no point in asking.

Paul went off to the game by himself. It was the same game Kylie went to, not long after the pregnancy test that had returned a positive result; it was the game from which her grandmother says she came home upset. We can assume the two of them met at the game and that she pushed him to leave Julie, and that he refused.

Paul returned to Illawong before the game had finished, very angry. Julie ran down the drive to meet him and came back distressed. He was in a filthy mood, abusing her for no reason.

'We've got to go,' she told her parents.

'What about dinner?' they said.

Some of Julie's old friends were coming around to see Bradley for the first time.

'He's cranky,' she said. 'I've got to go.' She grabbed Bradley and left the house.

When she'd gone, Kevin said to Jenene, 'Did you see the look on her face? She looked so scared.' He called Julie that night to see what had happened. She told him Paul had seen someone at the football he didn't like, so he'd left early. The story didn't make much sense. The Sydney Football Stadium is a big place, big enough to get away from someone you don't like and still watch a game. Paul seemed to have become even more erratic than before. Following this incident, Jenene began to note examples of his unusual behaviour in a diary.

On 11 May Paul received the phone call from Rebekkah Craig. Julie listened to his side of the conversation and could tell something was wrong. When he hung up, she asked what was happening and he said it was about the Kylie girl: 'I did some work with her for the police and she's gone missing— they just wanted to know if I'd heard from her.' He explained he had to go up to Gosford on 17 May to make a statement.

In the middle of the afternoon on 16 May, Paul was about

to drive Julie and Bradley to her parents' place, where they were to have dinner. As they were leaving the house, he put two family photo albums into the car.

'Why are you giving me these?' asked Julie.

'To show your parents.'

'They've already seen them.'

Paul left them in the car anyway and drove over to Illawong, where he dropped Julie and Bradley off, saying he was going to find his mother at the Engadine RSL to see if he could borrow some money: they were broke and out of nappies for the baby. He didn't return in time, so Julie and her parents started dinner without him. At 7.00 p.m. someone rang Julie from the Bankstown Police Station to say there'd been a fire at her house and that Paul had been taken to hospital. Julie was distraught, concerned about their house and belongings, and about Paul. She called his parents and told them the news, and learned that they hadn't seen Paul that afternoon, at the Engadine RSL or anywhere else. Ron and June came by at 8.30 p.m. and gave Julie a lift to Bankstown Hospital.

When they arrived, Paul didn't look too bad and joined Julie for a cigarette outside. He said two men had broken in and set the fire. He told her a dramatic story about his scuffle with one of the men, and how the place had filled with smoke after they'd left and he'd had to break his way out.

Paul was discharged soon after and the couple went to Bankstown Police Station to make statements. Julie told the police what Paul had said to her, and she learned that their pet cockatiel was alive. At least, she thought, the people who'd hurt Paul had been nice enough to take the bird outside before setting fire to the house.

A week later, Julie was talking on the phone to a friend who was a police officer. The friend was at work and had access to the COPS database, and he read her the report on the fire. It mentioned that Kylie Labouchadiere had allegedly been there. Later, Julie told Paul this and asked why he hadn't said anything about Kylie before. He said, 'I couldn't tell you what was going on because they threatened yours and Bradley's lives if I told you anything.'

At this stage, Julie was trying to keep her marriage together and still had some feelings for her husband, despite his trying ways. She believed his story about Kylie and the fire, and felt angry that another woman had been prepared to burn all Bradley's things. But she was also angry with Paul for having given her a false account, leading her to make a wrong statement to police. As always, there were limits to what she would do for him.

'I was trying to look after you and Bradley,' Paul said. 'Do you know how hard it was for me not telling you? Part of the reason I didn't tell you is because you're so jealous.'

Maybe in other circumstances Julie would have wondered why Paul would think she'd be jealous of Kylie. But at the time she had other things on her mind, trying to cope with the fire and sorting out where they were going to live. In any case, by now Paul's behaviour could be so odd that it was easier for her to switch off and just concentrate on the demands of her young baby.

Later he said to her, 'Can you go to a pay phone, ring Crime Stoppers [a police contact line], tell them you're Kylie and say that you're safe and don't want to be found.'

She said, 'No, Paul, because they can trace calls.'

'Oh, forget it, then,' he said. 'I'll get someone else to do it.'

They moved in with his parents at Yarrawarrah, where he talked continually about the fire as part of a pattern of victimisation by corrupt police. The fantasy grew with each telling and he convinced his parents of its truth. But Julie questioned it, and after a month she had an argument with her father-in-law that was so bad that she moved back to her parents' home. Although it was not clear at the time, this marked the beginning of the end of their marriage.

Julie still visited Paul with Bradley, and later that year, in October, he came out with the most disturbing thing he'd ever said to her. It started with a vague comment: 'You don't have to worry anymore—I've taken care of things and you're safe.'

'What do you mean?'

'Geoff Lowe organised for the Aboriginal guy from the house fire to kill Bradley and you,' he said. 'Kylie told me what time it was going to happen, so I sat up at the car park at the top of Menai High near the sports fields. I saw Lowe's car pull up down near the tennis courts and drive off again, then I saw the Aboriginal male—Lowe had dropped him there. I caught up with him as he was walking across the oval and killed him, and then I rang my uncle Alan and told him that I was in a spot of bother. He said he'd meet me at the oval, he arrived about an hour and a half later and we took the body up to Mooney Mooney and buried it under Mooney Mooney Bridge.'

Julie told Paul she didn't believe him (and there is no evidence Alan did anything like this), and he said, 'Don't ask Alan, he won't tell you anything. If you don't believe me, I'll take you and show you the body.'

This remarkable conversation ended when some of Paul's friends arrived. Julie dismissed it at the time. Eventually, she would ask herself, as others who heard Wilkinson's ravings have asked, whether it was all false or whether some of it described what he'd done to Kylie. Apart from anything else, the way an unnamed Aboriginal man kept cropping up in his stories was odd.

Much later, Julie would also ask herself why she'd stayed with Paul through all this stuff. But the weirdness had crept up on her over a long period. She was like the frog which is gradually boiled in water: if the change takes long enough, you can forget what's normal and lose your capacity to respond as you might once have done. There was also a fear of Paul. Maybe a certain wildness had been part of his initial attraction for her, but it had become fear, although she tried to ignore it. But it kept her with him longer than she should have stayed. She says now that for a long time the fear stopped her from allowing herself to even think about how bad he might be.

In October 2004, Paul was arrested outside the Engadine RSL. He'd been thrown out and was being aggressive to the bouncers, yelling and shirtless. It was a night of confusion, not least because, by coincidence, one of the officers who turned up to deal with the incident was Geoff Lowe. Paul had never met Lowe before. Now, when he realised who he was, he went off. He started to scream and accused Lowe of rape in front of the small crowd that had gathered.

Around midnight, Kevin and Jenene were woken by a call from police asking where Julie was. Apparently, she'd been at the RSL with Paul but had disappeared. The call came from the police station, and Kevin could hear June Wilkinson going on in the background. He told the police Julie wasn't there: it turned out that instead of following Paul to the station, she'd gone back to Yarrawarrah, where Ron had been looking after Bradley. At the police station, Paul was charged and allowed to go home.

The next month, on Melbourne Cup Day, Julie and Bradley were at Illawong while Paul and his parents celebrated at the Arncliffe RSL. Julie called him a few times that morning, and again after the big race to see if he'd had a win. His phone was off so she called his mum, who started to abuse her. Paul had disappeared and June believed it was Julie's fault, saying she and Paul must have had a big argument. He might be dead in a gutter somewhere. Julie brushed this off: it was typical Wilkinson talk and there hadn't even been an argument. A few hours later, Julie got through to Paul, who told her he was in Dubbo. He said he had no idea how he'd got there.

In fact, he'd won some money and on impulse had gone to the airport and taken a flight to Dubbo, where he was staying with relatives. Bradley's birthday was coming up, and Julie had to buy Paul a ticket back so he would be there for the occasion. He and his parents came over to Illawong on 18 November to celebrate the boy's first year.

By early 2005, Julie and Paul hadn't lived together for months. He still wasn't working and they were having rows all the time. This was disturbing for Bradley, who was the centre of Julie's emotional life. He needed a stable home to grow up in and Paul was incapable of providing one. At last, she summoned the courage to make their separation permanent. When she told her parents what she'd decided, Kevin was happier than he'd been in a long time.

On 6 February 2005 Julie told Paul she wanted a divorce. The next day Jenene answered a knock on the door to find two women who identified themselves as officers from the Department of Community Services and said they had come to investigate a phone complaint. It was a bit embarrassing: one officer was a client of Jenene's dry-cleaning business. They asked to speak to Julie and told her they'd received a complaint that she'd been abusing her child. She began to cry and rang Paul to tell him what was going on. Then she sat down in the lounge room with the officials, who went through the allegations they'd received. Bradley was toddling around the room and it was obvious he was healthy and unharmed, unmarked by the cigarette burns the officials had been told to expect. They said they'd guessed it was a fictitious complaint: extreme abuse of the sort the caller had described rarely goes unnoticed for eighteen months, which is how long the caller said Julie had been mistreating her child.

Paul turned up just five minutes after Julie rang him, along with his mother. This was odd, because the Wilkinsons' house was half an hour's drive away. The officials said the complaint had come in the day before, a Sunday, and been classed as urgent. The caller had said that if they didn't act immediately, he would go to the media. Paul always talked about going to the media over things that upset him: so far as Jenene was concerned, it was his catchcry. When the DoCS officials had gone, Paul said Geoff Lowe must have made the call. Julie replied that the officials had told her police might get a recording of the call and try to identify the caller. Paul didn't seem too happy with this idea.

On 5 March he called Julie to say he was going to Dubbo to live and needed a lift to the station. She went to Yarrawarrah, and as they were driving to Sutherland Railway Station, he announced that if she divorced him he would kill her. Julie was distressed and the fear of Paul's capacity for violence she had always suppressed came flooding to the surface. After she dropped him off she rang Jenene and asked her to call Paul's mother. Jenene rang June and realised she was at the club: the sound of poker machines was in the background. Jenene said she was going to the police to report the death threat but June begged her not to, explaining that Paul was on a good-behaviour bond because of the business at the RSL. If Jenene reported him, he would end up in jail. Jenene said she didn't care anymore.

When Julie came home she was still very upset and called Mark Polley at Bankstown detectives to tell him about the death threat. She chose to call him because he'd talked to her at the time of the house fire. As soon as she'd finished with Polley, her phone rang. It was another police officer, saying Paul had just called the emergency services centre, which takes triple-0 calls from the public. Paul had said that unless Julie met him right away, he would kill himself. The police came around and arranged for Julie to go to the place where Paul was, following her in an unmarked car. When she found Paul they picked him up and took him to the psychiatric ward at Sutherland Hospital. He was released the next day after the experts decided he wasn't really suicidal: he'd been making it up.

The drama went on for a long time, as Julie continued to see Paul frequently. In some ways, there wasn't much change in the nature of their relationship after the separation, given the amount of time they'd already spent apart on account of the alleged death threats. He still sent her text messages about his preoccupations and insisted on seeing her, often to get cigarettes or money. She says she went along with this partly because she feared what he'd do if she declined, and partly because she believed he had a right to see his son.

At about this time, Paul found out about another man Julie had had a relationship with before she met him, and as usual he hit the roof. They were driving through Jannali together and Paul raised his hand as though to hit her. She stopped the car in the middle of the road and told him to get out, but he wouldn't. Julie jumped out and saw a woman walking her dog, and asked her to call the police. Sensing a domestic, the woman shook her head and kept walking, and Paul got out of the car. Julie jumped back in and locked the doors; Paul was furious, yelling that if she drove off, he'd kill her.

On Tuesday 15 March 2005 the traffic lights incident referred to before occurred. Julie and Paul were driving along the Princes Highway in her parents' blue Hyundai Lantra and pulled up at lights, waiting to turn right into the Old Princes Highway. Next to them was a white Suburu Brumby utility, and to Paul's surprise the driver was Geoff Lowe. It was not a great coincidence they should find themselves next to each other: Lowe lived in Loftus, the suburb next to Paul's parents, and the highway was the main road connecting both places to the rest of Sydney.

Paul claimed that Lowe saw him and yelled, 'Keep your fucking mouth shut, otherwise I am going to kill you.' Paul told police and the complaint was investigated by Detective Acting Sergeant Andrew Ryan at Miranda Police Station, who rang Julie and asked her about the incident. Her memory was different. Paul had been swearing and carrying on, trying to get her to look at the white Suburu. She'd recognised Lowe but he hadn't even seen them: he had just sat looking ahead, waiting for the lights to change. Paul was yelling out abuse—'Cunt! Dog-fucker!'—but the windows were closed, and when the vehicles moved off, Lowe still hadn't noticed them. Julie had dropped Paul at his parents' house in Yarrawarrah and turned around to drive back. At Loftus she received a call from Paul, telling her to go to Sutherland Police Station. She drove there and waited for Paul to arrive. When he turned up he had Ron and June with him, and he told Julie to support his story of Geoff Lowe threatening them at the lights.

'I'm not going to lie for you,' she said when she realised he was going to make a complaint. 'I have to take Bradley home.' She left the police station.

Julie didn't tell much of this to Detective Ryan because she was scared of Paul. She just said she'd been in the car, sitting in the passenger seat, so she was closest to Lowe and hadn't heard any threat. She asked him not to tell Paul what she'd said, as this would cause problems for her.

Ryan wrote to Lowe to inform him of the complaint, and Lowe said he had not even known he was next to Wilkinson on the day in question. He told Ryan about the rape allegations Wilkinson had made to the police minister's office in

2001 and expressed concern that there would be more false complaints in the future.

Ryan called Wilkinson and, without referring to Julie's comments, said the complaint was being rejected. Wilkinson was clearly unhappy and accused Ryan of protecting Lowe (who was also stationed at Miranda). In June, Ryan advised the complaints-management team, 'It would not surprise me if the complainant makes further attempts to complain about Sergeant Lowe or other members of the NSW Police Service given his knowledge of the system and recent experience with the service.' He suggested that Wilkinson be assessed as a vexatious complainant. This didn't happen.

As we have seen, a few weeks later, in July 2005, Wilkinson went to the PIC with his nightmarish claim that Lowe had killed Kylie. Julie knew nothing of this until September, when Paul gave her a copy of the nine-page statement he had given the commission. They discussed it after she read it, and he added a detail that was not in the statement: he said Lowe had given him a choice between raping Kylie and stabbing her.

'I chose to stab her—I stabbed her four times,' Wilkinson said to Julie, 'because raping her would be too much like what happened to you.'

Julie just looked at him, not for a minute believing it, thinking this was just another of his crazy stories.

But the stories were getting worse.

By late 2005, the investigation into Kylie's death was heating up again. Since November the police had been intercepting

Wilkinson's phone calls, and Glenn Smith was thinking seriously about talking to Julie. Early in the investigation, Houlahan and Craig had decided against approaching people close to Wilkinson, because they knew they'd tell him about the sort of questions being asked, which would enable him to prepare mentally for their next contact with him. But it seemed from the calls they were listening to that while Julie still talked with Wilkinson, she didn't have much sympathy for him anymore. Her role in the relationship now seemed to be as the recipient of his increasingly emotional rants.

Wilkinson also had many phone conversations with the woman named Cheryl Kaulfuss, telling her he knew where Kylie's body was but had chosen not to tell the PIC in order to see how they'd react. He said his barrister and Ray Jackson, a support person from the Indigenous Social Justice Association, wanted him to tell the police where the body was, but he wouldn't until he had 'some sort of guarantee'.

The pressure was clearly telling on him, but he continued to cling to the notion that he could wriggle out of it by implicating Lowe and getting some sort of indemnity for his own role in (he claimed) burying Kylie in the Royal National Park. On 13 December he told Kaulfuss, 'The big thing is, if they want to come and grab me, then come and grab me. But at the end of the day, you don't scratch my back, I won't scratch yours, and it's their family that's not going to know where she is.'

Wilkinson told Julie she could expect a visit from the cops before too long, and he renewed his pressure on her to change her 2001 diary by adding a mention of being raped. Julie later told police, 'Paul has said on several occasions, "If

you do the diary it will strengthen my story about that cunt."
When Paul says "that cunt" he is referring to Geoff Lowe, as
this is how Paul always refers to Geoff Lowe.'

Julie continued to resist these requests, and Wilkinson's
behaviour deteriorated. He would call and demand money
and cigarettes, and threaten to come to her parents' house
and make a scene if she didn't oblige. Finally, she began to
consider the unthinkable: that he might have had an affair
with Kylie Labouchardiere. And maybe worse. By December
2005, Julie's desire to know the truth finally became stronger
than her fear of Paul; she called the police and said she wanted
to talk.

She was put on to Glenn Smith, who said it was a coincidence to hear from her. He'd been planning to ring her that
afternoon.

Julie was twenty-five, the same age Kylie would have been
had she still been alive—five years younger than Wilkinson.
Glenn Smith and Rebekkah Craig interviewed her at Menai
Police Station, and early on she asked what they thought had
happened to Kylie. They said they thought Paul had murdered her. As the detectives went through their questions, she
started to see her life over the past few years in a new light.
She felt shattered, not just that Paul had betrayed her but that
her son might turn out to have a murderer as a father. Julie
asked the detectives if they thought Paul had been having an
affair with Kylie. They told her she was pregnant at the time
she disappeared, almost certainly with his baby. Julie began
to cry.

In retrospect, Julie seems to have been gullible for a long time, believing stories such as the threats to her life that had forced her out of her house so often. Other people were gullible, too, most notably Sean, with his belief in Kylie's stories about the police work Wilkinson was doing and which she was supposedly engaged in. Kylie was gullible herself. We will never know the extent to which she believed Wilkinson's stories, but her behaviour while still with Sean indicates she believed at least some. In other cases she helped create them—for example, the death threats she wrote, and almost certainly the story about her alleged rape by Gary.

Of course, it takes two people to create an effective lie: one to tell and one to believe. Chronic liars know this and are adept at surrounding themselves with people who are prepared to believe their lies. This does not necessarily mean these people are gullible from the start. Sometimes a liar will start off by being honest in a relationship and introduce the lies gradually. Their partner will accept the lies because by then they are committed to the relationship, maybe because of love or a child. Sometimes lies are believed in a weak moment, to avoid conflict, and pushed to the back of the mind. Sometimes deceit can become part of the fabric of a relationship, hardly noticed anymore. This seems to have been the case with Wilkinson and Julie. Some of what he said was amazing stuff, but what was new? Julie and her parents had stopped taking Paul seriously long ago. As she now told the detectives, 'He just comes out with things sometimes.'

Something else he'd come out with was an observation about a car they'd passed at Loftus Railway Station that belonged to the wife of Geoff Lowe: 'That's that dog's wife's car,' he'd said. Glenn Smith found this disturbing: for Wilkinson to know this, it was likely he'd been watching Lowe's house.

The police asked Julie about a sledgehammer Wilkinson had borrowed from her parents' house and returned a few weeks after Kylie disappeared. Julie didn't know why he'd taken it: 'He was definitely not the handyman type.' It was another mystery—in this case, despite forensic examination of the implement, it would be one that was never solved.

Smith and Craig spent two full days with Julie, learning all they could about Wilkinson. Although the information filled in a lot of gaps, they were disappointed to realise that she knew nothing that put them much closer to being able to charge him. As it turned out, her greatest value was that she was still in touch with Paul. Over the coming years she was able to keep them up to date on his state of mind. Now she knew what he'd done, she was keen to do what she could to help Kylie's parents. As a parent herself, she felt sorry for what they must be going through.

Someone else the detectives spoke with in December 2005 was Wilkinson's uncle Alan, whom he'd rung the night Kylie disappeared. Alan Wilkinson lived on Karool Road, along Mooney Mooney Creek almost under the F3 bridge. A Vietnam veteran of average height with short dark hair, he was known in the area as a tough man who liked a drink. His nickname was Rambo. His house, perched on poles up a steep driveway, overlooked the creek, which despite its name is a fairly broad tidal river. Just below the house he kept a blue houseboat, with a tinnie tied up to it, and on occasion took off for a few days up Mullet Creek, to get away from things.

The detectives went up the steep drive and found a somewhat decrepit dwelling with building materials scattered around the yard. When Alan Wilkinson answered the door, they asked him to come to the station to make a formal statement.

Craig said, 'If you've got nothing to hide, it's pretty simple, just come and speak to us.'

'I don't know,' said Alan. 'I want to get a lawyer.'

'Go for it. All we want to do is get an explanation [of the phone call]. Your name's come up.'

When Alan Wilkinson arrived at Gosford a few days later, he told Smith that Rebekkah's words the other day had caused him to drink two cases of beer and jump in the creek. Possibly he shared his nephew's dislike of women in authority. He claimed to have no memory of the call Paul Wilkinson had made on the night of 28 April 2004, saying that he'd been away from home at some event related to Anzac Day, although he couldn't remember the details. The detectives were interested in Alan Wilkinson: he couldn't prove where he was that night, and phone records suggested he'd actually been at home, or nearby, when Kylie disappeared.

Meanwhile, the phone tap on Wilkinson's mobile continued. On Boxing Day he told Cheryl Kaulfuss, 'You go and investigate Geoff Lowe, and then you'll make a connection between 2001 [Wilkinson's delusion that Lowe had raped Julie] to this incident now [Kylie's death], and that'll prove that he's aggressive, and that it's in his nature to do it.' Then his story about the grave changed and he said, 'It's so unfortunate that I cannot remember the exact location . . . in the Royal National Park.' And yet twenty minutes later he texted her: 'the following is HALK co-ordinates 2 a location 26E 29N in the event of death & only death a cousin will ring u with the otha half.' These manic texts and phone conversations had become important in maintaining his delusions.

In January 2006 he texted Julie: 'I tried my best with them 2 kill me, I begged em 2 kill me 2 ensure safety 4 u and KING [his name for Bradley].' He told her that Geoff Lowe would be so angry if he talked that 'You might end up in the National Park, just like Kylie'.

In late January, Wilkinson told Kaulfuss he'd been contacted by the forensic specialist hired by his lawyers, who wanted to go out with him to look for the body again. He said he could no longer remember where it was. On 31 January he sent a text to Julie that combined all his fantasies about Geoff Lowe: 'I c what he did 2 her, I c the gun in my chest, I c the fire surroundin me, I c my version of what they did 2 u. Mostly the murder Julie it was vicious sadistic.'

There was one last person the detectives had to speak to for their case against Wilkinson. Although convinced his allegations against Geoff Lowe were nonsense, they had to be investigated, and so they arranged to interview Lowe in early 2006. It would be the first time anyone had talked to him officially about the details of Wilkinson's six-month-old allegation that he had killed Kylie Labouchardiere.

SETTING UP GEOFF

What Paul Wilkinson did to Geoff Lowe almost beggars belief. The others whose lives he damaged were at least connected with him, either directly or through their close relationships with Kylie or Julie. But Wilkinson had never met Lowe when he accused him of rape and murder. His hatred of the man stemmed from his possessiveness of Julie and his dislike of police officers in general, and blossomed into the macabre attempt to frame him for Kylie's murder.

Geoff Lowe was a uniformed sergeant at Miranda in 2006, and did not look like a crazed killer and rapist. When I met him later I found a mild-mannered man of below average size. In fact, although his father was a policeman too, Geoff had never thought he'd be accepted into the force because of its physical requirements: at sixty-four kilograms, he was simply too small. But in 1983 his application was successful and he soon found he loved the job and was good at it. He enjoyed the camaraderie, being part of a brotherhood of men and women who had to look after each other, no matter who they were. Much of a shift in the early years was spent driving around in a truck with a colleague, sharing your life's experiences to help pass the time. The next day it was the same thing, but often with a completely different person. And then there was cop humour, that take on the world that only someone else who's been through the same experiences can understand. Geoff also liked the knowledge that he was serving the community. Whether people were grateful or not, he knew he was doing a good thing, making a difference every day he went to work.

In 2001 Geoff had a long-term girlfriend named Sue. During a break in their relationship, he had a very brief sexual fling with Julie Thurecht. He got back together with Sue and they married in March 2005, and settled down happily in Geoff's house in Loftus, towards the southern end of the Shire. It was a modest, pleasant place right at the end of yet another dead-end street running into the bush. Like many houses in the street, it was made of weatherboard. It had a green tin roof and was shaded by big trees, overlooking a reserve maintained by volunteers. Geoff regarded it as his dream home, the place where he would bring up his children one day.

When he became a sergeant and moved to Miranda at the end of 2004, he knew Julie had married Paul Wilkinson. Geoff says Wilkinson had a reputation in the Shire among police, but as a client rather than a colleague. Sometimes he would get into trouble in pubs and clubs so they had to be called, and when this happened he would try to use his job to get special treatment. The fact he was an ACLO placed them in a tricky situation. They wanted to help him but he was also a pain in the arse.

In early 2002, soon after he sent his birthday text message with the sexual reference to Julie, Geoff received half a dozen anonymous phone calls with threats such as the intention to cut his throat. In an early call, the speaker used the term 'Pre-88', which referred to a police superannuation scheme. This made it almost certain the caller was with the police, and Geoff tried to think which colleague would want to abuse him like this. Later the caller mentioned the name 'Julie', which narrowed the field considerably. The calls came to Geoff's private mobile, which he figured Paul Wilkinson could have got from Julie Thurecht's phone. He kept a record of the times and dates of the calls. Finally, Wilkinson rang while his phone was off and left a long, abusive message. Geoff took this and the other information to his superiors, who arranged to have a check done on the source of the recorded message. It had been made from a public phone box on the Central Coast, not far from where Wilkinson and Julie were living at the time. Police management decided not to pursue the matter and Geoff changed his phone number.

In October 2004 Geoff met Paul Wilkinson for the only time. He was at work and was called to a job at the Engadine RSL Club, on the night Wilkinson had been ejected and (as described earlier) was carrying on outside. Geoff was in the second or third car to arrive, and found two officers restraining an Aboriginal man who had his shirt off. Geoff got out of the car, and a moment later the man started calling out his name, yelling, 'Get Senior Constable Lowe here.'

Geoff walked towards the man and racked his memory, thinking maybe he'd encountered the bloke before at some domestic incident. But nothing came to mind. When he reached the group, Wilkinson asked to speak to him around the corner.

'No, mate,' Geoff said. 'If you want to speak to me, just say whatever you've got to say here.'

To his surprise, Wilkinson proceeded to yell out that Geoff had once raped his wife.

'What?' said Geoff.

It was the first time he'd heard the allegation. There was a crowd of onlookers, and as he stared at their faces Geoff recognised one as Julie Thurecht. As soon as she saw him looking at her, she turned and ran off.

Wilkinson continued to hurl abuse at Geoff, until he was handcuffed and put in the back of a police truck. Members of his family were nearby, and they started to yell insults too, one of them using the word 'rapist'. Geoff found the completely unexpected incident incomprehensible. It was painful to be accused of rape, and even worse to have it done in public, in front of his colleagues. He was suddenly in some kind of twilight zone.

Gradually, though, the memory faded, and Geoff hadn't thought too much about Paul Wilkinson in a while when he was rung in April 2005 by Detective Andrew Ryan, who said he was investigating the complaint Wilkinson had just made about the incident at the traffic lights. As we've seen, the complaint went nowhere because Julie refused to support Wilkinson's version of the event. But after the threatening phone calls of 2002 and the incident at the Engadine RSL in

2004, it had a big impact on Geoff and his wife, Sue. She in particular became seriously scared of Paul Wilkinson, who they found was living at his parents' place, only five minutes' drive from their house. As the traffic lights allegation showed, he knew what sort of car Geoff drove.

Geoff complained about this history of harassment to his management team at Miranda. There had now been three incidents in almost three years. He asked that Wilkinson be charged with some sort of offence, or at least be recorded as a vexatious complainant. Nothing was done, so Geoff took the first of many steps for his own protection by changing the number plates on his car. This was not the end of the world, but he resented having to do it because his old plates were personalised and much-loved. He'd been given them as a twenty-first birthday present by an aunt who did this for all her nephews and nieces: it was a modest family tradition. Wilkinson was starting to affect the way Geoff lived his life.

Worse was to come. In mid-2005, Geoff was told he was being investigated yet again, because of a new and very serious complaint, a Category One. He was given no other details— not even the name of the complainant—which is standard procedure, but it added to his stress. Assuming Wilkinson had struck again (he was right: this was the murder allegation made to the PIC), he complained to his superiors about this latest example of harassment. He was told the complaint process would have to take its course. It occurred to him that Wilkinson was using his knowledge of the police complaints systems to exert emotional pressure on him; he would be fully aware of the stress caused by the drawn-out, secretive nature of the procedures involved. Had Geoff been anything other than a cop, Wilkinson would not have had this hold on him.

In December 2005 there was yet another strange coincidence. Geoff was out one night, and Sue—who by this point didn't like being at home by herself, from fear Wilkinson might call—had gone with friends to a nightclub in Cronulla. There she began a conversation with a stranger on the dance floor. This turned out to be Julie Thurecht. When Julie realised who Sue was, she said she used to know Geoff but had lost touch. Sue recognised Julie's name. Geoff—fortunately—had told her about their brief fling. Now Julie said she had something important to tell him, and Sue gave her his number.

The next night, Julie came to their house and gave them a copy of the nine-page statement Wilkinson had given the Police Integrity Commission six months earlier, accusing Geoff of the horrific murder of Kylie and other serious crimes. The Lowes were astonished and distressed. When Julie had gone, Geoff rang the duty officer at Miranda, who came over that night. He advised Geoff to show the document to the officer investigating the Category One complaint, which he did.

For weeks over Christmas and into January 2006, Geoff heard nothing about the matter from anyone in the police service. Sue and he were now very worried about their safety: from the PIC statement, it was obvious there was something seriously wrong with Wilkinson, who had a burning hatred of Geoff and lived in the next suburb.

Finally, on 9 February 2006, Geoff was interviewed by Glenn Smith and Andrew Waterman at the Sutherland Police

Station. Waterman was there to provide senior oversight, given that Lowe was a fellow officer.

Geoff denied every allegation Wilkinson had made to the PIC and said, 'I believe that for whatever reason, Paul Wilkinson is either jealous or resentful of any relationship I had with Julie a long time before Julie had even met him. Why he has this hatred towards me I have absolutely no idea. This bloke has dead-set made my life a living hell for the last couple of years. I've had to change my phone, I've had to sell my car, my wife's car. My wife is living in dread because I'm a shift worker and sometimes at night she's at home alone, she's just out of her mind sometimes that this bloke's going to come around.' He said he felt sorry for Julie because 'I know that she split up with him now and I would hate, if I was a female, to have an ex-husband like that who's just—he just seems to have some serious anger management issues'.

After the interview, the detectives visited Geoff's home and took away items of clothing resembling those Wilkinson said Geoff had worn while killing Kylie: five red and white St George football jerseys and two pairs of black tracksuit pants. They were later examined by a forensic expert and no traces of blood were found on them.

Geoff learned two terrifying things from talking to the Homicide detectives. The first was that Wilkinson, apart from all his other problems, was probably the murderer of Kylie Labouchardiere. He was, in other words, capable of extreme violence. The second was that he had been watching Sue at Loftus Railway Station on her way to work. He knew her car, her registration number and the time she caught the train.

The detectives urged him to pass on this information to his superiors, which he did; he was told that the police could put an alarm in his house. He said he already had an alarm but that Sue and he couldn't turn it on because they had two cats that kept triggering it. Geoff says the superior suggested they get rid of the cats.

Sue's fear increased when she learned that Wilkinson had been watching her, and she started altering her travel times and arrangements. She was in a continual state of anxiety, scared if she saw an Aboriginal male about Wilkinson's age when she was by herself. Whenever Geoff was on night shift, she would stay with friends. When they were apart, Geoff was always concerned for her safety. Finally, as Geoff's superiors continued—in his view—to ignore their concerns, the couple decided they had to move to get further away from Wilkinson. It was a tough decision, and they bitterly resented being forced out of their home as a result of Geoff's job. (He believed the PIC allegations had been triggered by his role in arresting Wilkinson at the Engadine RSL.) So they rented out their house and in June 2006 moved to a place in Helensburgh, just to the south of Sydney. Geoff asked the police service for financial assistance for the move, on the grounds that it was a forced relocation. He says his superiors refused, arguing that his problems with Wilkinson stemmed from his sexual relationship with Julie and not from his work as a police officer.

By now the detectives knew that Paul Wilkinson was a chronic liar, indeed a fantasist. They strongly suspected he had killed Kylie Labouchardiere twenty-two months ago. But although they had a large amount of material, they still knew nothing about what had happened immediately after Wilkinson had met Kylie soon after 9.00 p.m. on 28 April 2004. All the pieces of evidence were like arrows pointing at those hours. As to what had happened then, it was a black hole. There was not one piece of forensic evidence.

Glenn Smith and Rebekkah Craig still wanted to find Kylie's body, which might provide that evidence, despite the time that had elapsed since her death. They continued to tap Wilkinson's phone, and in February 2006 Julie asked him why he wouldn't take the police to Kylie's body. Surely, she said, Geoff Lowe's DNA would be found on it, and this would support his version of how she'd been killed. Wilkinson's reply was one of the most chilling of his texts recorded by police.

'That evidence u referring 2 lasts 4–5 days only b4 being lost,' he texted her. 'Everybody has reasons 4 hiding a crime. Mine is the family can live not knowing where and why 4 What they hav don. Call me cruel, call me nasty and YES Id agree, howeva my knowledge ISNT goin 2 b theres. It will hurt them NOT me. It WONT b there the DNA, BE TOLD RITE . . . And Im NOT goin 2, her family can live their lives in misery 4 all I care FUCK THEM. Weapon they can hav, her NO.'

These vicious references to Kylie's family are difficult to make sense of. Wilkinson had never met Carol or John or Michael or Leanne. He had no reason to dislike, let alone hurt, them.

The word 'theres' in the text is ambiguous. It could mean

the family but probably refers to the police, because sixteen minutes later Wilkinson sent Julie another text: 'The weapon they can hav, hopefully they do themselves ova with it the MONGREL DOGS.' What was this weapon, if indeed it existed? Was it the fictional one he'd claimed Lowe had used or was it one he'd used himself? As with so much Wilkinson said, the detectives had no idea what was true and what was not.

On 13 February, Julie, despite police warnings to be careful when with Paul, asked him if she could visit the grave, and he texted back: 'Fine. Ill show u.' But he didn't—not then, any-way. He was using his knowledge of the grave site to taunt Julie, just as he'd used it to bignote himself to the PIC and would later use it to taunt lawyers and the police and the courts. In the end, it would be the only thing he had that anyone wanted.

Wilkinson seems to have guessed that his phone was being tapped, as he dropped in puzzles and even messages for the police. Once Julie was asked by Smith and Craig to visit Menai Police Station to listen to some intercepts to clarify a few things. Suddenly she heard Wilkinson ranting, 'You pox-ridden slut, Rebekkah!' It wasn't the only time he'd inserted abuse of Craig into his conversation.

Smith observed, tongue in cheek, 'I didn't get a mention.'

On 20 February 2006, Wilkinson asked Julie to bring Brad-ley up to see him at his parents' holiday house on the Central Coast. When she arrived and they were alone, he told her that Geoff Lowe had ruined his life and talked about Lowe killing Kylie.

'I know where the murder weapon is,' he said. 'When I decide to give it to the police it will prove my innocence.'

'Where is it?'

'There is a creek that runs down beside Geoff Lowe's house—at the creek there is two big pipes, the murder weapon is about halfway along one of them, wrapped in a rag and put in a plastic bag.'

'How do you know?'

'I followed Geoff home and watched him put it there.'

This was new. As Paul seemed in the mood for disclosures, she asked about the body of the Aboriginal man he'd once told her he'd killed and buried under Mooney Mooney Bridge.

'I've moved him,' he said. 'That slut Rebekkah and Pace have been to Alan's four times. I think they think [Kylie's] buried there, so I moved him in case they let the dogs out down there and they pick up a scent.'

'How did you move him?'

'Alan's car.'

'So he knows as well?'

'No, Alan was down south and I know where he keeps the spare keys.'

'Where did you move him to?'

'I'm not telling, 'cause if the police turn up the heat on you, you'll crumble and lag me in.'

'I can't believe you think I'll do that.'

The next day Julie reported this conversation to police, who searched near Geoff Lowe's house at Loftus. Five metres from the driveway, a steep track plunges into the nature reserve and then splits, with one branch crossing a watercourse coming down from the street. Two pipes run under the track at this point, one of concrete and one of metal. It was here that Wilkinson said Geoff had hidden the knife with which he'd killed Kylie. The police did not find a knife.

The pipes cannot be seen from the street, so to know their location Wilkinson must have explored the bushland around Geoff's house.

Wilkinson continued to try to keep his hold over Julie, even pretending to tell her where a large quantity of drug money was buried. On 23 February he texted some coordinates: '26W 49S from the manly theme song its your. Workout the theme song & what that means locationaly and u a filthy rich woman. My departin gift 2 u.' Later that day he added: 'I shouldv said when u hit 26W walk 200m left til u get euc three with my teams name knifed in2 it on the stump, 3 metres rite of stump 1-1.5m down. On sons life it's the truth.' Julie could not have used the information even if she'd wanted to, as it made no sense at all to her.

The reference to a 'departin gift' suggests Wilkinson felt the police were closing in on him. His ravings were becoming increasingly erratic.

Glenn Smith was frustrated by the lack of firm information and decided to get an undercover officer to befriend Wilkinson, in the hope they might develop a relationship and Wilkinson would tell him where Kylie was buried. It was not a strong hope, but by this point the investigation had pretty well exhausted all other options. Smith and Craig and the undercover officer, whose name for this operation was Brad, decided he should claim to be making a film about police corruption. Brad was provided with a recording device and had a number of meetings with Wilkinson.

One conversation occurred on 14 March 2006 at the United Services Club in Sutherland. Wilkinson told Brad about his work history, how he started at Redfern and went on secondment to Malabar to help the ACLO there, who was 'having problems with the community and they weren't trusting him and they'd give him a bit of curry every time he went out to do a job so I just went across there to sort of stabilise things out there'.

Then he returned to Redfern, where he was stabbed in 1999 and went off work for eight months. He returned and in October 2001 was bitten on the hand by a junkie. 'We got him back to the charge room and he started laughing at me and I said, "What the fuck are you laughing at?" He said, "I've got hepatitis A through Z and I've got HIV."'

Brad: 'Oh yeah, that would've given you a bit of stress.'

Wilkinson: 'After that I went a bit, went a bit funny.'

Then he had another twelve months off work. He said he had no support at all from the police: it was just, 'Oh, okay, we'll put you down on HOD [hurt on duty] and we'll see you when we see you.' Finally he went back because he was sick of 'turning on the fuckin' news every night and seeing Redfern and all the kids getting portrayed as little criminals, which they are, but with wrongly, wrongfully bloody portrayed.' But, he continued, 'nothing had changed. Redfern's always going to be Redfern, that's for sure.'

The transcript of the conversation with Brad reads like a summary of Wilkinson's parallel universe. You can see how he'd knitted all his resentments and the killing of Kylie together into a version of events that put him at the centre, as a victim. It's an extraordinary and elaborate fabrication, and you can see why Geoff Lowe, who'd become entangled in part of it, talked about being in the twilight zone.

And yet whatever else Wilkinson was, he was smart enough to have killed someone and, several years after the event, to have got away with it so far. But however smart he was, he couldn't let go of what he'd done, which would have been the smartest thing of all. In his conversation with Brad—most of which was a series of monologues—he kept coming back to it, but in different forms, as though he could change the past with words, as long as he kept talking.

An important part of his imaginary world was still his continuing delusion about Julie's rape by Geoff Lowe. He told Brad how this complaint had gone nowhere, just like the complaint about Lowe threatening him at the traffic lights. When the officer who'd investigated that rang to give him the result, Wilkinson said he'd responded, 'Let me guess, Geoff Lowe's sitting in the office with you now, isn't he? . . . I guarantee you he's in there. He's under the desk, giving you a blow job.'

As usual, at least in his own mind, Wilkinson's problems stemmed from his superiors' refusal to take him seriously.

'If they were charged in 2001 for the complaint that I went to, to the police minister about,' he told Brad, 'it would have been all over and done with. If it wasn't such a boys' club and it is that corrupt, they didn't want nothing to do with it. So you've come down the track five years on, what have you got? You got a major drug syndicate, still a lot more people than what it originally was . . . you got more crime in, in, in, in the sense of, um, well, it's a crime to pass a sheila around from bloke to bloke . . . It's certainly a crime to fuckin' kill someone.'

Brad: 'Mm.'

Wilkinson: 'So, instead of being stopped at the rape—'

Brad: 'It could have been avoided.'

Wilkinson: 'These other things should not have happened.'

Brad: 'Mm.'

Wilkinson: 'And who's responsible for all that? The commissioner is responsible for it, as is the police commissioner, as is the, the, the, as is [former premier] Bob Carr at the time, 'cause he was in charge of New South Wales. You cannot tell me that he did not know about it.'

Wilkinson's raving was full of bravado. After he'd witnessed Lowe kill Kylie, he said, 'I packed Julie up, Bradley up, me boy.'

Brad: 'Yep.'

Wilkinson: 'We took the fuckin', took off up to Walgett, where Mum comes from.'

Brad: 'Yeah.'

Wilkinson: ''Cause I thought, you know, they might come up here, there's a lot of wild blackfellas here and they won't get past them.'

Brad: 'Yeah.'

Wilkinson: 'So we've basically been running, running ever since.'

Brad: 'Right.'

Wilkinson: 'Until I made a decision, I said to them, "I'm not going to run no more."'

Brad: 'Yeah.'

Wilkinson: 'If they want to kill me, they can go ahead and fuckin' kill me. I don't care.'

At times you wonder if one reason for Wilkinson's stories, repeated again and again to different listeners, was a need to inject some excitement into his own boring existence, now that he was unemployed and living with his parents. It was as though he was trying to turn his life into an action movie, in which he played the heroic survivor.

As to why he had not shown the PIC where Kylie was buried, he told Brad: 'I said to them, "You can have the location providing two things happen . . . no Sutherland police are involved, no Miranda police are involved . . . But I knew that they were going to fuck it up, they were gunna piss [in] me pocket . . . So I gave them a location which was a false location . . . and I'm glad I did that. Sutherland and Miranda police were there . . . mate, the, the, the place was swarming with Sutherland and Miranda coppers.'

Brad: 'So you know the location, do you? The real location?'

Wilkinson: 'Yeah. Nobody's going to get it until I get some satisfaction from [the] PIC.'

At the end of the meeting with Brad, Wilkinson said he thought his phones might be being tapped. So, he said, 'Well, what we, what, what I, what I do with people now, we, um, from now on your name is Fred.'

Brad: 'Right.'

Wilkinson: 'Right, and, and—'

Brad: 'So when I ring, you just call me Fred?'

Wilkinson: 'And my name, my name's Fred. We're both Fred.'

Brad: 'All right.'

It seems that Brad, to encourage Wilkinson's interest, offered him money for his appearance in the documentary he said he was making. On 4 April Wilkinson texted him: 'If I may ask a favour, may receive $2000 2day 2 escape on my return & body . . . Body location and full story u keep the agreed $15,000. Ill expose all 4 fuck-all Im desperate chap 2 get away til im 100% fit & out of harms way.'

The next day he texted: 'Maandowie Creek Loftus is a piece 2 the puzzle. In the event anything should go wrong or u fail 2 get a msg from me check that spot out.'

But despite all this teasing, he never told Brad where Kylie was buried.

After six months working in the Homicide Squad office, Smith and Craig did not have enough evidence to charge Wilkinson. It was now two years since Kylie had disappeared. The bosses brought them back to Gosford, where they were expected to do other work as well. Totally committed to the job of finding enough evidence to charge Kylie's killer, Smith resented this.

Whenever he wanted to do something using police money, Smith would have to argue his case with Ray North-cote, Gosford's Local Area Manager. It got to the stage where Smith would walk into his office and Northcote would say, 'No,' before he'd even heard the request. But it was just a joke: Smith would haggle and always got what was needed in the end.

One thing in Smith and Craig's favour was that the Wilkinson investigation was so unusual it captured the interest of many people in the job. Craig remembers that she would explain what she was doing and fellow officers would be intrigued. This helped them jump the queue sometimes when asking for assistance from different sections of the police service. A lot of people were aware of the ACLO who'd gone off the rails, who had killed and so far got away with it.

But even so, time was running out. One day a boss talked to Smith about the Wilkinson investigation and said, 'We're going to have to put a sunset clause on this.'

'Excuse me?'

'Just lock him up. He'll probably throw his hands up.'

'No,' Smith said with exasperation. 'He's got a solicitor and barrister. There's no way he'll plead guilty on what we've got. We actually have to prove this.'

The detectives had submitted a report to the coroner saying they believed Kylie was dead. This meant that at some point they would have to either charge someone or ask the coroner to conduct an inquest, at which they would need to demonstrate that they'd exhausted all avenues of inquiry. Smith didn't believe they'd yet reached that point, but it was getting close. Before long, a decision would have to be made, and it would be terrible if, due to insufficient evidence with which to charge Wilkinson, the matter went to a coronial inquest and a finding that Kylie had been killed by a person or persons unknown.

To Brad and others during these months, Wilkinson kept dropping hints about the grave. One text to Cheryl Kaulfuss read: 'Fun Funs Zwanzig /Zwolf/Elf/Drie. Fritag Nacht.

K translate and keep 4 your records. It's a co-ordinate.' On 18 May 2006, Paul and Julie met up, and in the car outside her parents' place he said, 'Do you want to see where Kylie is?'

Again ignoring the warning she'd been given by the detectives, Julie said, 'Yes.'

He directed her to drive to the Royal National Park. They went down the Meadows Fire Trail in a lonely part of the park, and according to Julie's memory, 'I noticed that Paul started to become tense. His face looked rigid and he looked pale . . . Paul always clenches his jaw when he is either tense or angry.' They stopped along the track and he told her this was the place where Kylie was buried.

Julie looked around and suddenly realised how isolated she was, alone with Paul in the middle of nowhere. Just the silence of the bush, broken by the calls of a few birds. But he didn't seem to realise how strange the situation was, so she did her best to remain calm and interested. They didn't stay for long. When she got home after dropping Paul off, she immediately called Rebekkah Craig.

On 30 May, Wilkinson told Julie he was meeting with police at Sutherland the next day to tell them where Kylie was buried. Over the next fortnight he changed his mind several times, until a second search for Kylie's grave finally started on 13 June—almost a year after the meeting at the PIC. Smith and Craig held a briefing at Sutherland Police Station with numerous officers from the Public Order and Riot Squad (which is used for work like this when there are no riots) and the Forensic Services Group. Smith was mildly optimistic, hoping Wilkinson was about to lead them to the body but aware that even if they found it, there might not be much of forensic value, two years after Kylie's death. He knew that a lot of bodies of murder victims are buried in a hurry, which means the graves are shallow and often disturbed within months by wild animals, with the bones being scattered over the surrounding area. This, as much as the decomposition of the flesh, limits what police can learn.

The search occurred in an area near the Meadows Fire Trail in the Royal National Park, but drew a blank. The next day another search took place along the Gundamaian Fire Trail, not far from where the search of August 2005 had been conducted. The police examined the ground for fifty metres on each side of two-and-a-half kilometres of trail—a big job—but again nothing was found. These searches involved thirty-four people and cost $26,852.

Wilkinson, who was still living at his parents' place just over the railway line from the national park, was not present, but as the search occurred he ranted to his various callers, telling one that police were pointing the finger at the wrong person, and another that he himself had now forgotten where the body was buried, so how could anyone else find the spot. On 16 June (when the searches were over) he told Cheryl Kaulfuss he could hear helicopters flying over the national park, and two days later he said the police weren't looking hard enough: who was to say he hadn't moved the body? Anyone with a fuckin' brain would have moved it.

Reading the transcripts of some of these calls, you're struck again by Wilkinson's success in surrounding himself with people prepared at least to tolerate, and often accept, his persistent delusions. In a way, they were like mirrors, although what they were reflecting was an imagined version of himself, one in which he was still a 'player' and not a man on the edge of madness, with the police closing in on him.

Later he said to Julie, referring to their drive to the national park in May, 'Don't think I took you to the right place, 'cause I knew you'd run to them [the police] . . . Those cunts [Lowe and his associates] are setting you up—if I give up the location you'll go down, as they've planted stuff.'

'Well,' Julie said, trying for the reasonable approach, 'I'll ring Gosford Detectives and tell them I'm being set up.'

But Paul had lost touch with reasonable. 'If you do that you'll bring yourself down.'

'How am I being set up?' she said.

'You don't need to know.'

In mid-2006 John Edwards left his position at Jobfind at Parramatta. The effort of being enthusiastic for job-seekers who needed him for inspiration, while his own life was falling apart, had become too much. He'd thought he'd been holding it together, but now, two years after Kylie's disappearance, he had to accept that he wasn't. He took a position with a plumbing company as general manager, embracing the challenge of turning a struggling business around. It was a job that needed a lot of commitment but did not require him to wear a smile every minute of the working day.

And yet although the detectives could not give John any details, the investigation was still making progress. On 27 June, Smith and Craig went to Marrickville Police Station and talked with an ACLO named Derek Wilson. He was a former colleague of Wilkinson (and Craig) and, like

Wilkinson, had given evidence to the parliamentary inquiry into the Redfern Riots. Wilson told the detectives he had once had a conversation with Wilkinson about meeting someone named Kylie at Sutherland Railway Station, but he couldn't recall when it had taken place.

After the formal interview had finished, Wilson said to Craig, 'Bek, come and have a cigarette with me.' Although not a smoker, she followed him outside, where he said, 'Did this girl have any money on her when she went missing?'

'She did, actually. Why's that?'

'Wilko had a lot of cash on him around that time. I'm talking thousands. It was around the time of TJ, after that some time. Mate, we hit it, pokies, drinkin', you know, he was spending a thousand dollars a day at least, and this went on for maybe a few weeks . . . We were drinkin' from morning 'til night, on the Keno . . .'

Craig said, 'Did Paul ever tell you where he got this money?'

'No, and I never asked, you know. I thought he got six numbers in the Keno. He made it very clear that Julie was not to know about the money.'

Wilson later made a formal statement, about how Wilkinson had gone on a gambling and drinking spree in early April. The detectives never found out how he had persuaded Kylie to give him the money, but it had almost certainly come from her. They found a text Wilkinson had sent her on 31 March 2004: 'I hav u now I WONT let u go and I WONT allow u 2 fail the tests set upon u howeva u r failing THIS IS DEFINATE LAST TEST.' It hints at how he manipulated her into borrowing $24,000 in the last months of her life, as part of her desperate effort to win his love.

Occasionally, the investigation threw up completely unexpected lines of inquiry, which led nowhere but involved further work. At one point there was attempted activity related to one of Kylie's bank accounts. The detectives discovered this was due to a criminal in Queensland named Jeffrey Cooper, who was a running a scam involving the bank accounts of missing persons. In September 2006 he was arrested and pleaded guilty to some sixty-five fraud offences involving the accounts of five missing people. He confessed that he had tried to transfer money out of one of Kylie's accounts, but without success.

Glenn Smith asked the police Missing Persons Unit to conduct standard searches to see if there was any trace of activity from Kylie. Some of these had been done when she first went missing, but that was now two years ago. Senior Constable Darren Conabeer checked with the Department of Immigration, Multicultural and Indigenous Affairs to see if she'd left the country. The surnames Labouchardiere, Edwards and Wilkinson were used, but no records were found. He checked with the major banks and building societies, with Centrelink and Medicare, other missing-persons units around the country and the electoral roll. He checked with the NSW Registry of Births, Deaths and Marriages. He also checked his own unit's database of unidentified bodies, or parts of bodies. Everywhere he looked he drew a blank, but this 'negative evidence' would be important if Wilkinson was ever to be put on trial for murder: it would be necessary to show that all reasonable efforts had been taken to see whether Kylie was alive.

Gradually, with months of hard work, the police were able

to eliminate each of Wilkinson's fantastic claims. He was an unusually deceitful and imaginative criminal, but he was up against one of the state's most enthusiastic young detectives in Glenn Smith, and in Andrew Waterman one of its most experienced. There was also Rebekkah Craig, who'd been there since the beginning and provided valuable continuity—although the investigation went on so long that she was to go on maternity leave twice. Wilkinson continued to confuse and sometimes baffle with his weird statements, but at the end of the day he was only one man, while those opposing him were many: Strike Force Bergin was backed by one of the largest and best-resourced police forces in the world. Paul Wilkinson had got away with an awful lot in his life, but it was all about to catch up with him.

For over a year Geoff Lowe had been asking his superiors for an official threat assessment of the risk posed by Wilkinson, making a pest of himself, he felt, and the experience added to his stress. He'd never been particularly self-assertive, never one for pushing himself forward or even fighting his own battles. Having to take on his superiors was an entirely new experience, and an unhappy one. His sense of the camaraderie of the police service began to weaken. Given its previous importance in his life, he found this unsettling.

The formal risk assessment was finally done in September 2006, and it was a disappointment. Geoff says it involved ticking boxes on a form, the process taking just five minutes. By this stage, the Lowes had moved to Helensburgh, so Wilkinson no longer knew where they lived. Partly for that reason, the threat was assessed as low. Despite the fact that the police force had now recognised that Geoff's wife had been stalked by a suspected murderer who had an obsessive hatred of her husband, nothing was done. Geoff says no senior officer ever approached him or Sue to talk about what they were going through.

By the end of 2006, Sue was pregnant and the couple could not afford two houses. They sold Loftus in a depressed property market. It was the latest blow in Paul Wilkinson's secret war against Geoff Lowe.

In August 2006, a year after he'd taken over the investigation, Glenn Smith made a big decision: at last there was enough evidence to charge Paul Wilkinson. The general case was that Kylie had been gone for over two years, and the only plausible explanation was that Wilkinson had killed her: Smith and Craig believed they now had enough evidence to disprove any other probability.

The next step involved writing a 'sufficiency of evidence' document, which, with other material, ran to several hundred pages. It was a huge job. Smith and Craig used the strike force room on the second floor of Gosford Police Station and covered three whiteboards with lists of the evidence that needed to go into the document. Andrew Waterman dropped by to look at what they had and suggested some other things that were needed, so even more evidence was obtained. Finally, it was ready.

What they had was a circumstantial case based on a hypothesis. Following the discovery of Kylie's pregnancy, they believed, Wilkinson had told her he would leave his family and move to Dubbo to live with her. She had left home on 28 April 2004 with the intention of meeting him at Sutherland Railway Station, from where they would travel to Dubbo. Wilkinson had met her at the station, and then killed her and disposed of her body at places unknown.

Evidence in support of this hypothesis included the facts that (proved by telephone records) the two had been in a close relationship for several months, that Kylie had been putting pressure on Wilkinson to leave his family, that she had recently learned she was pregnant with what was almost certainly his child, that she'd embarked on a major change in her life (indicated by the big announcement she'd promised her family but not delivered a few days before she disappeared, and by the cards she'd left in her room for her sister and grandmother), and that she'd moved her possessions to Dubbo (a city with which she had no connection, although Wilkinson did).

There was also the large amount of money she'd borrowed from family and financial institutions before her disappearance, over a period when Wilkinson had much more money than usual. Smith and Craig believed that this money had been given to him by Kylie, possibly for the purpose of establishing a new life in Dubbo. If this was right, the fact that he'd spent the money on gambling and a holiday for his family suggested he'd had no intention of going away with Kylie.

One problem with the hypothesis, apart from the absence of forensic evidence or a crime scene, was that Kylie had not told anyone she was going to live with Paul Wilkinson; he also denied any intention of moving to Dubbo with her. Smith and Craig suspected that Kylie had not told her family about the move on Wilkinson's instructions. If true, this fitted with their suspicion that he had lied to her about wanting to move to Dubbo. This raised the question of just how he'd thought the matter would be resolved, when he arranged to meet her at Sutherland Railway Station on the night of 28 April 2004. Possibly he'd intended to kill her all along. Or possibly he hadn't thought it through and killed her on the spur of the moment, maybe because they had an argument when he told her he wasn't coming after all and she threatened to tell Julie about their relationship and her pregnancy.

The next step for the detectives was to obtain the agreement of the state's Office of the Director of Public Prosecutions that they did indeed have enough evidence. This was necessary before Wilkinson could be charged, and it proved to be a fraught process. Initially, the brief was sent to the Gosford office of the DPP, but when the lawyers there saw Wilkinson's claims of Geoff Lowe's involvement in Kylie's death, they forwarded the document to their head office in Sydney. There it was handled by a solicitor named Janis Watson-Wood, the manager of Group Six, which deals with cases involving allegations of police misconduct and corruption. After considering the brief, Watson-Wood wrote a 130-page report in which she said it was one of the most bizarre matters she'd ever come across. She then moved to another position, and the solicitor who took over the matter, Meaghan Fleeton, referred the brief to a senior Crown prosecutor for an opinion. He decided the case was just too circumstantial—the chance of obtaining a conviction at trial was remote. Therefore it should not proceed.

Smith was immensely disappointed by the decision. It felt like a slap in the face after all the police effort, some of it done in his free time as he'd become increasingly involved in the pursuit of Wilkinson. At this point it looked like Paul Wilkinson was going to get away with murder. However, Fleeton decided to seek another opinion, and a meeting was arranged for 4 April 2007 between Smith, Fleeton and the deputy DPP, David Frearson SC. Andrew Waterman would be there too, along with Janis Watson-Wood. Smith was on tenterhooks. For practical purposes, this was pretty much the end: if Frearson turned him down, the case would go to the coroner.

On Saturday 31 March, Smith went to his office in Gosford and wondered what else he could do to strengthen his case at next week's meeting. It was a warm day; elsewhere on the Coast, people were outdoors in the sun, on the beaches and the sports fields, with friends at barbecues, playing with their kids in parks. Smith's own family was at home without him, just as they'd been on the day two weeks after he'd been posted to Gosford, when he'd been given his first murder investigation. That seemed a long time ago, and here he was, in the office again on a weekend, still trying to solve his second one.

He began going through the investigation's extensive records on the police database, not looking for anything in particular but hoping there might be something they'd overlooked during the past three years. It was not much of a hope, but he had nothing better to do. He looked for a long time, and then, to his surprise, found something: it was an 'exhibit matrix', a list of items taken from Kylie's room at her grandmother's house when it had been searched in the weeks after her disappearance, long before Smith became involved in the investigation. On that list was a mobile phone with a different number to the one she'd had with her when she went missing, which had never been found.

A second phone?

Smith went to the big cupboard where material from the investigation was stored. The phone was there, a Nokia. It was probably an old mobile that had been replaced by the one Kylie had used so frequently in the months before her disappearance. But still, it ought to be checked.

Back in the detectives' office he recharged the phone and tried to get into its memory, but found it was blocked by a request for a password, or PUK code. There was a standard procedure for this sort of thing, and he made a request for the code number to Telstra, using the police IASK computer program.

On Tuesday, the code having arrived, Smith took it and the phone to the police Electronic Evidence Branch in Sydney. The unit is expert in obtaining information from phones and other devices, using procedures that ensure the results can be presented as evidence in court. After a wait, Smith was handed a seventeen-page report of information found in the phone's memory. With growing excitement, he saw that it contained numerous text messages that had been sent between Kylie and Paul Wilkinson—she must have used this phone sometimes even after she got the new one. Some of the texts were useful in filling in small gaps. But one text message, from Wilkinson to Kylie, was more than just interesting: it was dynamite. What Smith now held in his hands was a piece of information that filled a major gap in the police case.

A week after Kylie had told Wilkinson she was pregnant, he had sent her this message: '2day & Wednesday then it's DB [Dubbo] u and I are 2getha 4eva.'

As far as Smith was concerned, it was the SMS equivalent of a smoking gun. It contradicted Wilkinson's claim that he had never been in a relationship with Kylie, and suggested he had lured her to Sutherland by promising they were going away together.

The next day, Smith walked into the DPP's office for the meeting and handed the downloaded text messages to Janis Watson-Wood, pointing to the one about Dubbo.

'This is pretty exciting,' she said.

Deputy DPP David Frearson came in soon after and they went over the evidence against Wilkinson.

Abruptly, Frearson said, 'So, why haven't you charged him yet?'

Smith was so surprised that it took a few seconds to realise what he'd just heard.

ARREST

Strike Force Bergin, like most homicide investigations, had been conducted in great secrecy. Geoff Lowe was among those who had no idea what was going on: all he knew was that Paul Wilkinson was still walking the streets and still posed a threat to himself and possibly his wife. In late 2006, having had Wilkinson's threat assessed as low by the police force, Sue and Geoff decided he should seek promotion to inspector level, in a job far from Sydney. They would get away from Wilkinson and start a new life.

Next year, Geoff applied for a position of Commissioned Officers rank for the first time. It was quite a step: the increase in both status and salary between sergeant and inspector is considerable. But he was an experienced officer who'd handled a lot of tense situations well: he'd been involved in the 'Strathfield Massacre' investigation, he'd had shotguns pointed at him, he'd been the General Duties Mobile Supervisor at

Cronulla during the revenge attacks after the riot in December 2005. With over two decades' experience, he was sure he'd make a good inspector, especially somewhere well away from Sydney.

He didn't know that soon Paul Wilkinson would no longer be a threat.

Glenn Smith's plan was to arrest Wilkinson on 17 April 2007, just before the third anniversary of Kylie's death. Usually on these occasions the police go in early, simply to be sure the person is at home. Smith arrived at Sutherland Police Station at 6.30 a.m., bringing a statement of facts he'd prepared and intended giving the court later that morning, after the arrest. He was joined by Andrew Waterman and Rebekkah Craig, who was on maternity leave (her second child had been born a few months earlier) but wanted to be there for the end. Also present were other homicide and local officers, including Ben Mang, who'd put in so much work over the previous year listening to Wilkinson's phone calls. Based on Wilkinson's pattern of phone use in recent weeks, they expected to find him in bed when they arrived at his parents'.

At 7.30 a.m. they drove to Yarrawarrah and surrounded the house. Smith walked up the concrete driveway and knocked on the front door, which was opened by June Wilkinson. He said he wanted to see Paul but she said he wasn't there. The detectives were dubious.

'Can we come in and have a look?' said Smith.

June allowed him inside and he saw she was telling the truth. Given his habits, Wilkinson's absence was a real puzzle.

Smith asked her to call Paul to find out where he was; she was so nervous that she had trouble using the phone.

Not finding Wilkinson at home was frustrating for the detectives, although more because they'd been denied the satisfaction of taking him by surprise than because they expected him to get away. They returned to the police station and Smith called him. It was the first time the two men had spoken. Wilkinson was cocky and refused to say where he was. (The police later learned he'd got up uncharacteristically early to repay some money to Julie so she could take Bradley to the Easter Show.) He said he'd come in to the police station later with his solicitor, Frances McGowan, but she wasn't available at the moment.

The next few hours involved various attempts to track Wilkinson down. Police were driving around the area trying to locate him while Smith maintained occasional phone contact. Wilkinson rang Julie to tell her what was happening and she panicked: she'd thought the police would let her know before the arrest so she could go away for a few days. Now she became terrified and called Smith to say she wanted to withdraw all her sworn statements. He told her that was not an option and sent some officers to her house, in case Wilkinson turned up. As the morning progressed, he rang Carol and John Edwards and told them what was going on.

Just after 2.00 p.m., Wilkinson arrived at Sutherland Police Station with his parents, his brother and Frances McGowan. He was wearing a baggy blue T-shirt and dark cargo pants, white socks and joggers, and clasping an empty Coke bottle. He had put on weight and his belly was visible beneath the T-shirt but he was still a good-looking man, with strong features and an intense gaze. In comparison, his parents—Ron with a pair of glasses hanging from a cord around his neck—were large, lost-looking people. Over the coming years, they would continue to believe in their son's innocence.

The detectives were out the back of the station, and Craig reluctantly decided not to be present when the arrest was made. The situation would be intense and she didn't want Wilkinson's dislike of her to flare up and interfere with what was about to happen. Smith and Mang went out to the foyer and saw Wilkinson and McGowan, a thin woman with long, dark hair, in a black dress. Wilkinson looked at them blankly.

Smith cleared his throat and said formally, 'Paul, I am Detective Senior Constable Glenn Smith from Gosford Detectives and this is Senior Constable Mang from Sutherland. Paul, you are under arrest for the murder of Kylie Labouchardiere. I must warn you that you are not obliged to say or do anything, as anything you do say or do will be taken down and may later be used in evidence. Do you understand that?'

'Yep,' said Paul Wilkinson, who seemed calm.

Smith searched him and then left the charge room while Wilkinson was read his rights by the custody officer. Smith returned and was told by McGowan that Wilkinson was exercising his right to silence. Smith recorded this and formally charged Paul Wilkinson with murder, and with the arson of the house in Picnic Point.

Later, they went across the road to Sutherland Local Court—the same place where, years before, Robert McCann had been convicted for his assault on Kylie's mother. Wilkinson applied for bail and was refused. McGowan criticised the police because their ten-page statement of facts, prepared the day before, claimed Wilkinson had been arrested at home. Smith was embarrassed to realise that after finding Wilkinson was not at the house that morning, he'd been so preoccupied with searching for him that he'd forgotten to amend the statement.

'Shoot me now,' he thought as he listened to McGowan.

The magistrate handed the statement back to the police to be corrected, which meant it was not available to the media then or when Wilkinson was brought before Central Local Court to make his formal bail application the next day. This is one of the reasons that the case, despite its many sensational aspects, received little public attention for a long time.

There was no police celebration following Wilkinson's arrest. By the time they'd finished with the court appearance and other matters that had to be attended to, it was dark and Smith walked out of the station alone to his car. He made the long drive home to the Coast, back across the Mooney Mooney Bridge. He felt a sense of achievement but it was mixed with anti-climax and just plain weariness. It had been a long day, and he knew a lot more hard work lay ahead, probably including a tough court battle, if Wilkinson was ever to be convicted. Today was good but it was only the first step. He got home late, as he had so often before, had a few beers in front of the television and went to bed.

The news that someone had been charged with Kylie's death was both devastating and consoling for her family. There is no such thing as closure for people who have lost a family member in this way, but there can be changes to the intensity of grief. Only now did some of the family accept that Kylie was dead.

Carol was shattered by the news. Leanne had to tell her own daughters, aged seven and ten, that their aunty was up with God. The children broke down and cried. They asked their mother questions—'Why did this happen?'—which she could not answer. For Leanne, the reactions of her children made it all much worse.

Glenn Smith rang John Edwards and told him what had happened. Until that moment, John had never been sure it was Wilkinson, had never fully accepted Kylie was gone. His thoughts had still been all over the place, wondering if Sean had had something to do with her disappearance or if Wilkinson might be hiding her because she'd learned too much about the death of TJ Hickey. But he could no longer believe these things, or any of the other theories he'd come up with over the past three terrible years.

'Mate,' Smith said, 'the facts are there.'

The detective couldn't tell him what those facts were, not yet, but John trusted him. He knew that it was over.

After Wilkinson's arrest, the DPP asked the police to do more to strengthen the Crown's case. This included reinterviewing witnesses and searching the grounds of the Kelvin Parade house (which, since the fire, had been repaired at a cost of $38,000) for Kylie's body. Further information came to light, including an intense relationship Wilkinson had had with another woman outside his marriage, just before he'd met Kylie. As so often with Wilkinson, the more you look, the more patterns emerge.

On 7 February 2008 a uniformed police officer, whom I will call Anna Simons, made a statement about this. Her story was fascinating because of its similarities with what we know of Wilkinson's relationship with Kylie. In December 2002, Simons, who was almost the same age as Kylie and Julie Thurecht, finished her trainee course at the police academy and was sent to Redfern Police Station, where she met Wilkinson. They soon became friendly as he advised her on how to handle the Aboriginal people she dealt with in the job.

'Wilkinson and I flirted during our friendship from the outset,' she said. 'I found him funny, charming, attractive and intelligent. He often made suggestive comments about my sexuality and I returned the banter . . . I was, like every probationary constable, under a lot of pressure to learn the intricacies of policing in a volatile, high profile command, while trying to fit in to the policing culture. Wilkinson was very friendly and supportive.' She realised he had a strong sexual appetite, and he used to comment on the attractiveness of their colleagues.

In September 2003, their friendship became more intimate, but still non-physical: 'I knew he was married at the time and his wife was pregnant, and I remember this concerned me, but I was attracted to him and, against my better judgement, I encouraged his advances.' He began to send her sexually explicit text messages several times a day and late into the night. These were things like 'U look hot today' and 'Ur so sexy in uniform', followed by 'I wanna put you over the desk. U get me hard just seeing u walk in.'

They met later that month to discuss their relationship. He wanted to have sex but she declined, because he'd told her he would not leave his wife. In October the text messages became more frequent, thirty or forty a day, and well into the night. Sometimes there were as many as eighty a day, messages like 'I want to fuck u so bad'. They agreed to meet again for a further talk, at Waverley Cemetery. 'I knew where that was,' Simons said in her statement, 'and remember thinking it was quite romantic at the time as Waverley Cemetery looks out over the ocean and is quite a beautiful spot.'

By now Wilkinson had been moved to Marrickville, and Simons told him she wanted to end the relationship. 'I'm not really comfortable, having a relationship with you when your wife is about to have a baby,' she said. 'It's wrong and I feel really bad about it.'

'I want to have you both,' Wilkinson said. 'I haven't had any in months and I want to fuck you so bad right now.'

She told him no, and the relationship faded over the next month or two, especially after Bradley was born on 18 November. Simons said Wilkinson told her he'd had sex with other people in recent months, including a man he met on Oxford Street in Darlinghurst. He also said he was thinking of moving to Dubbo with his wife and child.

A few weeks later, Wilkinson went into Sutherland Hospital for tests and met Kylie.

In January 2008, Wilkinson's barrister, Terry Healey, told Glenn Smith that his client was prepared to reveal more information about Kylie's disappearance, and on 13 February he was brought up to Gosford Police Station. Apparently, Kylie was not buried in the Royal National Park after all, but somewhere north of Sydney.

But when the Corrective Services van reached Gosford, Wilkinson refused to get out. Smith went out to the vehicle and had a conversation with him. Wilkinson claimed he'd never agreed to come to Gosford, where 'that fat slut Rebekkah Craig works', and didn't want to be there because it had a 'connection' with Redfern. He refused to leave the van, and in the end it took him back to Sydney.

Two days later, Smith conducted a recorded interview with Wilkinson at the Metropolitan Reception and Remand Centre at Silverwater. There he heard a new story: Julie had been present at Kylie's murder. In fact, she had assisted: 'Geoff Lowe choked Kylie whilst Julie held her legs,' said Wilkinson. In this version, Julie had driven him to the murder location, following Geoff Lowe's vehicle. After Kylie was dead, he had dug a grave and Lowe had put the body in, after which Wilkinson had replaced the soil. Julie had stood by, smoking Winfield Blue cigarettes, and as Wilkinson dug he told her she was 'a mongrel, dog, cunt'.

Wilkinson said he was not prepared to say why Kylie had been killed, except that it involved 'a fellow by the name of Sheik Fazi who goes to the Lakemba Mosque' and had something to do with the theft of army rocket-launchers: 'I've actually handled one of those rocket-launchers . . . we are dealing with people that don't give a fuck.' (A number of rocket-launchers had been stolen from the military, and the possibility they were in the hands of terrorists was the subject of occasional speculation in the media at the time.)

On 18 March, Wilkinson, having again announced he was prepared to reveal the location of the grave, was brought back to Gosford Police Station. Smith, who had assembled a search team, noted he was in an 'aggressive and agitated state'. He said the body was at Mooney Mooney, under the big freeway bridge. This was interesting: it was where Wilkinson's uncle Alan lived.

Glenn Smith legally recorded this and later conversations on a portable recorder, and they provide a fascinating insight into Wilkinson's frame of mind. He now said, 'You wanna go down there, let's go down there, but you start pullin' ya finger out and start being a fuckin' proper copper. Start doin' the right thing and don't bring that fat slut near me either.'

Smith: 'Paul, I'm not bringing her, I told you before that we wouldn't be bringing her . . .'

Wilkinson: 'I'm not happy with you either.'

Smith: 'Paul, let's just get what you want to do today over and done with. I've just got to organise the guys from the video unit . . .'

Wilkinson: 'Don't bring 'em.'

Smith: 'The video unit?'

Wilkinson: 'Don't bring them . . .'

Smith: 'All right, you're going to have to go in the van with the guys, and we'll follow you down there.'

Wilkinson: 'Fuckin' ridiculous.'

Smith was angry at Wilkinson's manner but kept his cool. He could see the humour in it—after all, Wilkinson was the one in handcuffs. They reached Karool Road at Mooney Mooney and drove past his uncle Alan's place and up to an area near the gigantic pylons that support the smooth white bridge far above. Wilkinson identified a spot where the grave might be. Then he suggested another place. Police went to work, clearing the ground and inspecting it with a cadaver dog and ground-penetrating radar. As Wilkinson watched the search, he raved about various matters, including his still unexplained hatred of Rebekkah Craig. He continued to try to play with Smith's mind, asking him where he thought the body was and taunting him with hints of knowledge. At one point he referred to the stolen rocket-launchers he'd mentioned the previous month: 'Let me tell you something, Glenn, it's not a matter of if there's gunna be terror attacks, it's a matter of when. And if you're pullin' my fuckin' chain and ya think I'm pissing in people's pocket, when it happens and if youse haven't done anything about it, it's gunna bite you on the arse, not me. I've given you every opportunity.' A few minutes later he said, 'Man, I know that you think that I'm a fuckin' lunatic and I'm way out there, but you put this in the media and people are gunna die.'

Then he started to go on about Julie, telling Smith he ought to 'start doin' something about that fuckin' ex-wife of mine'. The fact that Smith hadn't chased up some of the things he'd previously told him about Julie enraged him. 'Why the fuck didn't youse do things right since the first place? If ya hadda started doin' it then I woulda given youse everything without fuckin' youse around. But now ya still fuckin' me around . . .'

Smith: 'I wasn't here, Paul [at the start] . . .'

Wilkinson (indicating his handcuffs): 'Damn lucky these are on.'

209

Smith: 'All right, Paul, I can see you're getting angry with me.'

Wilkinson: 'Getting angry with ya, I'm livid with ya, I'd love to snot ya . . . Don't you think it's a little bizarre, that bang I'm in custody and Julie's got a new bloke? Don't you find, don't you find all of that side of things sort of strange?'

After some more raving, he said, 'Why do you think I fucked youse around from day one? Why do you think I did that?'

Smith: 'I don't know, Paul.'

Wilkinson: 'Well, ask me.'

Smith: 'Well, why did you stuff the original guys around from day one?'

Wilkinson: 'Because I'm sittin' in Bankstown detectives' office, Rebekkah Craig walks in with the look of fury on her face. "What the fuck's wrong with you, Rebekkah?"

' "You tell me."

' "Well, fuck you too, Rebekkah." That was it, she walked in with an attitude, because she took it personal because we used to work together at Redfern. She took it personal.'

They kept chatting and Wilkinson learned for the first time about the undercover operative, Brad.

Wilkinson: 'Who the fuck is [that]?'

Smith: 'He's an undercover operative . . .'

Wilkinson: 'Where did I meet him?'

Smith: 'At the SUS Club . . .'

Wilkinson: 'You're a sneaky cunt.'

On the whole, Smith didn't enjoy these walks in the bush with Wilkinson; this search proved as futile as all the rest. But for a moment he felt happy.

★

As the four-year anniversary of Kylie's disappearance approached, John Edwards wanted to do something to remind the family of Kylie's life rather than her death. He came up with the idea of a memorial service where the family and others would talk of their memories of her. Some family members criticised the idea but it went ahead on 26 April 2008, at the Terrigal Senior Citizens Club on the Coast.

John organised the whole thing, including a celebrant and a poem to be read at the event, and the hire of the hall and provision of food. Even the preparations were a deeply emotional experience: it took him a month to prepare a memorial card because he would break down and lose his capacity to focus on the task. On the day, a slide show of photos of Kylie was shown, the poem was read and there were speeches from most members of the family. Michael was overseas but John arranged for him to ring up and talk to the family. Afterwards, those there told John the experience had been worthwhile.

Despite this, John's grief remained intense, and because of this he had difficulties handling his job at the plumbing company. In July he resigned. He'd done good things there, tripling the company's turnover in his first year, but the responsibility and effort had become more than he could bear, given his emotional state. When walking in a crowd, he would see a young woman and think it was Kylie, and have to repress the desire to shout his daughter's name and run up to her. When he was home, every time the phone rang he hoped it was her.

He found he couldn't work anymore and spent a lot of time just sitting around at home, thinking about Kylie and the time it was taking to get Paul Wilkinson to trial. By

February 2009 he was no longer able to meet the mortgage repayments on his home in Lurnea and lost the house.

Geoff Lowe decided to persist with his plan to leave Sydney, even after Wilkinson was arrested. He and Sue had lost their house in Loftus and were keen to get away from an area that reminded them of the bad times they'd been through. Geoff's second attempt at promotion was successful, and he won an inspector's position at a dream posting, Lismore in the sub-tropical north of the state. His marks were excellent in all the categories involving objective tests. The only problem was his score based on 'management team comments', which had been embarrassingly low: just thirty-five out of 100. He believed this bore no relation to his actual performance but was a result of resentment because of all the trouble he'd caused at Miranda by complaining about his managers' inaction over Paul Wilkinson. However, the low score was not enough to stop him getting the job, and in February 2008 Sue and he and their young child moved to a small farm on the north coast, to make a fresh start.

But Geoff's luck turned again. There were five appeals against his promotion, which was almost unprecedented for a man of his seniority, with twenty-five years in the job. In June 2008 one of them was successful, thanks in large part to Geoff's low score based on the management team comments. Paul Wilkinson had struck again, this time indirectly.

Geoff took two days' stress leave after learning of the successful appeal, the first such leave he'd taken since the Wilkinson business began. He was a sergeant once more, and for Sue this was the last straw. She was living with a small child in relative isolation in the country, far away from her old friends and community. If Geoff had remained an inspector, with more status and money, things might have been better, but now they were back where they'd started and hundreds of kilometres from home. Six months later, she took their child back down south, and her marriage to Geoff was over.

Thanks to Paul Wilkinson, Geoff Lowe had lost his peace of mind, his home, his promotion and his family.

CONFESSION

Like most people charged with a serious crime, Wilkinson had a committal hearing at a local court, where the Crown's case was presented to a magistrate to determine if there was enough evidence to proceed to trial. It was a so-called 'paper committal' and no witnesses were called. Wilkinson pleaded not guilty to murdering Kylie, and the magistrate decided the case was strong enough to be put to a jury. A trial date was set for late in 2008, and Smith worked busily to obtain yet more information for the lawyers. He sought an update from the Missing Persons Unit, where the checks of two years ago were repeated. Once again nothing was found.

As the trial approached, Wilkinson's lawyers requested a psychiatric report from Olav Nielssen, an experienced forensic psychiatrist. They wanted to see if there were any mental-health issues that might affect their client's capacity to stand trial. Clearly, Wilkinson was not normal—but was he actually mad?

Nielssen interviewed Wilkinson at Silverwater and in his report described him as 'a man of Aboriginal appearance who was clean shaven with close cropped hair. He polished a pair of glasses in a theatrical way and held them in front of him for the duration of the interview. He was initially suspicious, reluctant to discuss aspects of his case, but soon became conspiratorial in his account of his knowledge and involvement in a range of criminal enterprises.'

Wilkinson told Nielssen he was unaware of any family history of psychiatric disorder, and had had few contacts with mental-health services. He had been stabbed with a syringe in 1999 and had started using drugs, although he would not specify which ones. He said he had been a 'big gambler', once losing $80,000 in a weekend on the horses.

Julie and he had formally divorced two weeks before.

Turning to his present situation, Wilkinson said, 'I am up against the government . . . strings will be pulled to make sure I get it [a guilty verdict].' He told a version of his story about Kylie's death at the hands of Geoff Lowe, and said that while he had known Kylie, the numerous texts and phone calls she'd received from his phone had actually been sent by someone else. As to the large sums of money Kylie had obtained just before she disappeared, he said these had been to pay off Geoff Lowe, a corrupt police officer who had raped Julie and then had an affair with her and fathered Bradley.

Nielssen concluded that Wilkinson's intelligence was in the normal range and his intellectual function was largely unimpaired. However, he held what seemed to be paranoid views regarding the police, the legal system and the government. 'Mr Wilkinson's presentation is unusual,' wrote the doctor, 'and it was not possible to make a firm psychiatric diagnosis on the basis of one interview without the benefit of corroborative information from a family member or someone who knew him well. However, on the basis of the information available, derived from the history elicited, his presentation during the interview and aspects of the case, I believe the most likely diagnosis is one of underlying psychotic illness presenting with grandiose claims and persecutory beliefs . . . I believe there are serious concerns about Mr Wilkinson's fitness for trial'.

The Crown sought its own report from another psychiatrist, who (as is not uncommon in this situation) disagreed with the opinion obtained by the defence and thought Wilkinson was fit to be tried. The disagreement between the experts would need to be resolved before the trial could commence.

Before going any further, it might be useful to reflect on those of Wilkinson's lies that had become major fantasies, and on how he had tried to tie them all together. Here is a summary.

1. Julie Thurecht was raped by policemen Geoff Lowe and a colleague in January 2001.
2. Policeman Mick Hollingsworth killed TJ Hickey on 14 February 2004.

3. Wilkinson and his family received death threats on and off from February 2003 to April 2004.
4. Wilkinson's house was burned down by Kylie and an Aboriginal man on 16 May 2004.
5. Kylie was killed by Geoff Lowe, and in a later version by Julie too, in the Royal National Park in April or May 2004.
6. Kylie was buried at various locations.

Lies are commonly used by people for practical purposes, to assist in doing wrong or covering up. Lie number three (the death threats), for example, was used to get Julie out of the house so Wilkinson could pursue his affair with Kylie, and possibly with Anna Simons before her. Number four (the fire) was intended to distract attention from himself as a suspect in Kylie's disappearance by suggesting she was still alive.

But in other cases, the motivation for the lie is less evident. Take number one, the rape of Julie. At first glance, there seems to be no reason for telling it. When Wilkinson found out she'd had a brief sexual fling with Lowe, and felt intensely jealous about this, he could simply have left her (they were not yet married). Instead, he stayed and created his lie about the rape. This might make some sense if he'd been passionately in love with her, but there is no evidence of this (although he did want to control her). What he seems to have been really passionate about was the story he had spun about Lowe.

This, and some of his other lies, might more usefully be called fantasies. They seem to have stemmed from a desire to create a sort of parallel world, one that suited his emotional requirements better than the world in which he actually had to live. Each of these fantasies spawned lies of its own, either spontaneously (eg. the Lowe traffic lights complaint) or because of Wilkinson's need to link things that really happened with his fantasy life (eg. blaming Lowe for Kylie's death). He was quite inventive when it came to joining his various fantasies together, which confused those around him and made the job of untangling them even more difficult for the detectives.

Part of the lying process for Wilkinson was a need to repeat a lie to others, to make it seem real by talking about it often. It is difficult to overestimate the strength of this compulsion, which did him no favours in the end. It was his statement to the Police Integrity Commission that led to the investigation into Kylie's disappearance being reinvigorated. It was his continued communication with Julie (even when he suspected she was relaying what he said to the police) that produced elements of the case against him. If he had simply kept quiet, he would be a free man today.

But he could not stay quiet, because he needed to give voice to his fantasies to keep them alive. And he wanted to keep them alive because his fantasies were more important to him than his real life. He lived in his stories.

The Crown prosecutor for the trial was John Kiely SC, a white-haired man with smooth skin and glasses, and a warm Australian accent. He was then in his late sixties and one of the most experienced prosecutors in New South Wales. He had grown up in Cowra, and from his father, a bookie on country tracks, he acquired a familiarity with a wide range of people and behaviours. On leaving school, he went into a seminary for four years, before deciding it was not for him and becoming a country solicitor.

He went to the bar after being involved in an unusual victory in a murder trial. A man had shot his de facto's father and then walked into the police station, handed over the shotgun and announced, 'I shot the cunt—he deserved it.' It was an unpromising start, but when the lawyers got to examine the weapon they found it was faulty, and this contributed to a successful defence of their client. Kiely thought this was pretty fascinating stuff.

In 1977, he and his family moved to Sydney's northern beaches and he soon had a thriving practice on the country circuit, as well as some industrial work for a union in Newcastle. In 1990 he decided it was time to ease back a bit—he'd been working six or seven days a week for years—and became a Crown prosecutor. The job involves only criminal cases—usually, after he rose through the ranks and became a deputy senior Crown prosecutor, murder trials in the Supreme Court. Kiely took silk in 1999.

He's done many famous trials. One was of state politician Barry Morris, convicted in 1992 of threatening to bomb the Blue Mountains City Council building. Another conviction was Lennie McPherson, often called Sydney's Mr Big, for assault. At the end of that trial, as Kiely was leaving the court, McPherson called to him, 'You'll be the death of me—I'll die in prison.' McPherson was right: he died in 1996, at Cessnock Gaol.

Kiely found a huge difference between being a defence counsel and a Crown prosecutor. In defence, there's no need to prove anything—you just need to break down the Crown case. But the stakes are much higher: if you lose, someone might go to jail for a very long time, and this pressure has got worse. When Kiely came to the bar, the sentence for murder was typically a non-parole period of ten years. Now it's about twice that.

Being a prosecutor is more disciplined: you have to prove the various elements of murder in a systematic and confined manner. The Crown must disclose its case to the defence before the trial begins; there is no obligation on the defence to do likewise. There is also an obligation on the Crown's part to assist the judge and ensure the trial is fair.

The Wilkinson case was unusual from the start, both because there was no body and because of its complexity. There were all the text messages, the burning of the house, the stories told to the PIC and the various searches for the grave. Working with DPP solicitor Helen Rallis, Kiely spent many weeks mastering the details of the police brief and working out how he would conduct the trial. This was a considerable intellectual challenge, although of course he'd done it many times before. It's been said that a barrister has a mind like a bathtub: with each new case you fill it up with knowledge, and when it's over you pull the plug and it all runs out. Then you put the plug back in and fill it up with the next one.

The trial was estimated to last six or seven weeks, with over a hundred witnesses due to be called. There was a need to prove that a relationship had existed between Wilkinson and Kylie, drawing on evidence such as the breakdown in their respective marriages. The burning of the house and Wilkinson's various allegations about Kylie's death would have to be described and explained in court. Then there was the mobile phone evidence, which has convicted many criminals and would play a central role here.

Kiely found it helpful, as he often did, to think of the forthcoming trial as a play, with various acts and scenes representing the different elements, all of which had to be conveyed to the jury in a way that would enable them to grasp the story of what had happened. This meant witnesses would need to be presented in the best order. It would all come together in the Crown's closing address to the jury, which for a barrister is the climax of a trial, when the main elements are drawn together, ideally in such a way that the jurors are convinced by the Crown's interpretation of those elements.

John, Carol and Leanne were kept in touch with the legal process by a DPP witness assistance officer, who was assigned to them for the extent of the trial. They spoke often with solicitor Helen Rallis, whose job involved not only supporting Kiely with the legal side of things but also liaising with everyone involved in the trial, including the police and the defence solicitor. John Kiely met with the family and explained what was going to happen. During the trial itself, he would have little time to speak with them, as all his attention would be consumed by running the case.

The trial was due to begin on 13 October 2008 before Justice Elizabeth Fullerton in the Supreme Court of New South

Wales. But on the first day of that month, Wilkinson protested that she should not sit because, before going to the bench, she'd been the counsel assisting the coroner at the inquest into the death of TJ Hickey. Wilkinson, of course, disagreed with the coroner's finding that the police did not kill Hickey. Fullerton stood aside and was replaced by Peter Johnson, a highly respected judge with a short grey beard and glasses.

On the morning of 13 October, John Kiely received some news from Helen Rallis. Wilkinson's lawyers had just told her that their client wished to change his plea: he was going to admit to killing Kylie. The announcement sent a shock through Kylie's family, who were sitting in the public gallery. Emotions of relief and anger, happiness and despair, swept over them, and for a moment they seemed to freeze.

Such last-minute confessions are actually not unusual. Accused people often wait until the eve of their trial to confess to a crime, in the faint hope something might change in their favour: maybe the Crown will propose a deal, or a vital witness for the prosecution will be run over by a bus. In the absence of such luck, they change their plea at the last minute because it gains them a discount off their sentence of about ten per cent. The state provides this reduction as an inducement, because a guilty plea removes the necessity for an expensive trial.

John Kiely was happy to hear what Wilkinson was proposing to do, but cautious. He wanted to make sure a plea of guilty would stick, and one thing that concerned him was whether Wilkinson was mentally capable of making the change. So he asked the judge to make a determination and

Johnson agreed. This would involve considering the evidence of the psychiatrists. And so the emotions of Kylie's family went on hold again.

As we have seen, Olav Nielssen had interviewed Wilkinson on behalf of the defence and raised a question about his fitness to be tried (that is, whether he was capable of giving instructions to his lawyers). This opinion had been countered by Stephen Allnutt, who had interviewed Wilkinson on behalf of the Crown. Allnutt had been provided with a great deal of material about Wilkinson, and his interview took place on 14 August. By that point, Wilkinson had been in jail for sixteen months and was taking anti-depressants for most of that time. He worked as a sweeper at Silverwater jail and kept to himself, because of a concern he said he had that police might arrange for someone to bash or kill him. Allnutt found Wilkinson to be well-groomed. He spoke clearly and maintained good eye contact, and 'denied any perceptual disturbances such as voices, visions, tastes or smells. He was not experiencing any messages from the TV, the radio or the newspaper.' He was guarded in his manner and concerned about the fact the psychiatrist had been hired by the Crown, but nevertheless he ran through most of his beliefs regarding Geoff Lowe and his own persecution by the police force and government.

Wilkinson told Allnutt he had suffered physical but not sexual abuse as a child. He said he had been stabbed in the stomach with a syringe in 1999 but that his superiors had refused to believe this. Despite that, he had taken six months off work and tried to kill himself in 2000 by taking a lot of pills. After that he had spent about $200 a week on cannabis and had also taken ecstasy, speed, cocaine and heroin.

The documents Allnutt had been given revealed that Wilkinson, despite what he'd told Olav Nielssen, had a history with the mental-health system, mainly connected with his long periods off work. In 2000 he was diagnosed with post-traumatic stress disorder, following the supposed stabbing the previous year, and in 2002 with depression. A psychiatric assessment in October 2002, after he had been bitten and off work for ten months, revealed a low mood: 'The impression was that he had anti-social traits, depression, post-traumatic stress disorder, alcohol and drug abuse, and blackouts of unknown cause . . . He was aggressive and violent towards his girlfriend, moody and withdrawn . . . He reported long periods of amnesia, odd behaviour and forgetfulness.' In the years following Kylie's disappearance, he had seen psychiatrists several times, and in 2005 presented in 'a depressed mood and was irritable and angry'. In March 2006 he had been diagnosed as having a major depressive disorder.

Allnutt decided that Wilkinson did manifest 'a paranoid condition' but 'manifests capacity to understand what he is charged with [and] the nature of the proceedings'. For this and other reasons, he concluded that Wilkinson was fit to stand trial. So now Justice Johnson had to decide between the psychiatrists' competing views.

Wilkinson was in court, looking thinner than when he'd been arrested—he'd lost about fifteen kilograms in prison—with his hair short and a moustache and small beard. Most prisoners dress up for court, but for every appearance Wilkinson would wear prison-issue green sloppy joe and trousers, and white Dunlop sandshoes.

Kylie's family were in court every day, apart from Michael,

who now lived overseas. John always wore a suit and tie and looked worn and sad, the big grin of his earlier years gone. When he first saw Wilkinson he felt angry, but also sympathetic for his parents and the things they had to listen to in court. He continued to be upset by Wilkinson's attitude towards his family, and his lies about the grave site. Once he thought about how he might jump from the public gallery into the body of the court and attack Wilkinson, but it was just a passing fancy.

Carol and Leanne travelled down from the Coast by train each time the court sat, making arrangements for time off work and, in Leanne's case, for the care of her children. These arrangements were complicated by the fact that the court sittings were irregular, with large gaps as the matter dragged over the lengthy Christmas break. Fortunately, both Carol's and Leanne's employers were understanding and helpful.

On some days in court, the women were accompanied by a DPP witness assistance officer, a woman from the Salvation Army, or Minouche Goubitz and Clare Blanch, members of the Homicide Victims Support Group. This is an organisation of people who have had a member of their own family killed.

Wilkinson's parents were there too: his father, whose expression gave nothing away, and his smaller and often angry-seeming mother. They were usually accompanied by a skinny Aboriginal woman who wore tops on which she had written words relating to various perceived injustices. She had a chesty cough and would sometimes shake her head indignantly at what was being said in the courtroom.

★

As it turned out, a battle between the two psychiatrists was not necessary on 13 October, because Nielssen interviewed Wilkinson that morning and determined 'that he is on balance fit for trial . . . Mr Wilkinson was able to provide a version of the events that was consistent with the account he gave you [that is, his lawyers] this morning and could form the basis of instructions in his defence.' Justice Johnson announced he was satisfied that the accused was fit to plead guilty to the charges of murder and arson. It was a moment of enormous significance for Kylie's family, who went home that afternoon tremendously relieved that they would not have to sit through a trial, and that Kylie's killer was finally known for sure and had been brought to justice.

The next day, Wilkinson formally confessed to killing Kylie, and gave a version of what had happened. It's a horrific account and, like much that Wilkinson expressed, needs to be regarded sceptically. This is what he wrote.

I, Paul James Wilkinson, in custody at the Supreme Court at Sydney, hereby instruct my counsel Terry Healey and instructing solicitor, Rochelle Macredie, as follows.

1. On 28.4.04 I had made arrang. to meet w. Kylie Labouchardiere @ Sutherland Rail/y Station @ about 9pm.

We had made arrange. to elope and go to Dubbo together to live.

Kylie and I had been in a romantic relationship for over 6 months. I was married @ time to Julie Thurecht and had a son Bradley. During the time of my relationship w. Kylie she had asked me to get rid of Julie and I believe that she meant to kill her. When I met Kylie @ the Sutherland Rlwy Station a little after 9pm 28.4.04 I put her suitcase in the boot of the car I was driving and I believed that we were heading for Dubbo. I knew that Kylie had made arrangement to send her belongings to Dubbo and as we travelled along she said to me, 'Can we go back to the Central Coast to pick up my digital camera as I've left it behind?' I said, 'Okay.'

I drove towards the Central Coast and turned off at the Hawkesbury River Bridge onto the Old Pacific Highway. Kylie and I became sexually aroused and one thing led to another and I stopped the car just past the Old Mooney Mooney Bridge and we made love.

During the intercourse she said to me, 'There was no need to come back up here for the camera. I just needed to get you away.' I said, 'What do [you] mean?' She said, 'If you're not going to have Julie killed then I will—I've already organised it.'

When she said this to me I lost it, I thought immediately of my son Bradley who would be w. his mother Julie and that some harm would come to him and I just lost it.

My penis was still inside her and I just lost it— I grabbed her by the throat and I was thinking 'You rotten fucking bitch' and I choked her w. my two hands around her throat but I did not intend to kill her. I thought I had been deceived and tricked.

I took my hands off her throat and then I felt Kylie go limp and I realised she might have lost consciousness and tried mouth to mouth and chest compression but she had died. I did not intend to kill her. I panicked and I turned the car around and drove south over the bridge, turned right up the fire trail for about half a kilometre. I stopped. Kylie was still in the back seat wearing only her top. I thought I would bury her in the bush.

I got out of the door and I had my clothes on and I went up the hill through the bush to where the houses are. I walked towards the houses—about 5 of them. I went into one of the yards, found a shovel and went back down to where I had parked the car. I dug a hole and before that I put her in a doona and I buried her. I think I may have bound her hands and feet with electrical tape but I'm not quite sure now.

I was in a very distressed state and I didn't know what to do.

I am very sorry for what I did to Kylie and I have been living and putting everyone else through a nightmare. I am very sorry for Kylie's parents and family as well as my own parents and family.

I did not intend to kill Kylie and I accept responsibility for her death.

I authorise this document by my counsel and solicitor to the Crown and Detective Glenn Smith.

I have authorised a copy of the plan I drew yesterday to be given to the Crown to where I buried Kylie.

[Signed by Wilkinson, Macredie and Healey]

14.10.08

After taking this statement, barrister Terence Healey appeared in court and told Justice Johnson that Wilkinson had confessed. He was staying in the cells below in order to 'maintain his current mental stability'. This followed what Healey had described the previous day as 'a small outburst' that had also led to Wilkinson's absence from the courtroom. Now Healey told the court that 'issues of diminished responsibility with substantial impairment may be a live issue in this case'. What this meant was that Wilkinson might be pleading guilty not to murder but to the lesser crime of manslaughter. Although he was fit to plead now, he would probably be claiming he had not been mentally fit when he killed Kylie four and a half years ago.

Healey said Wilkinson was prepared to be interviewed by Detective Glenn Smith and would be cooperating in the matter of locating Kylie's grave. He had already drawn a map indicating quite precisely where Kylie was buried, just off Karool Road in Mooney Mooney—the general area police had already searched.

Glenn Smith didn't think much of Wilkinson's confession. He suspected he was trying to portray the murder as a crime of passion when it had been nothing of the sort. But he interviewed Wilkinson, and the area at Mooney Mooney was searched that afternoon and again the next day, 15 October, at a cost of $10,000. No trace of a grave was found.

Smith reported these results to Wilkinson at Silverwater the next day. This interview was as frustrating as every other conversation he had had with Wilkinson, a mixture of obvious lies, paranoia and details that just might be true. He took him over the events of 28 April again, and the contents of his confession, including his claim that Kylie had said Julie was to be killed. Wilkinson said, 'I've asked you before to go through the [text] messages and you'll find a message on there where Kylie has said that if I don't kill Julie then she will do it.'

Smith: 'We can't get SMS messages retrospectively . . . We can only get them as they happen.'

Wilkinson [who probably knew this]: 'Well, that doesn't help, does it?'

Wilkinson said the reason he'd been going away with Kylie was because Julie had told him Bradley was not his son. Despite this, he insisted it was his deep feelings for the boy that had led him to kill Kylie. In the past, his lies had tended to be more consistent than this.

Smith asked whether he'd been angry when he'd killed Kylie.

Wilkinson: 'Anger because of the boy.'

Smith: 'Yeah . . .'

Wilkinson: 'If something was going to happen to Julie, so be it.'

Smith: 'Yeah.'

Wilkinson: 'But just don't do it when, when the boy's around.'

Wilkinson said it had been very dark and he could not recall exactly where the grave was. Smith explained their failure to find anything the day before: 'A cadaver dog detected something . . . We dug that area up, there's nothing there. Cadaver dogs are hit and miss, you know?'

Wilkinson: 'I thought they were accurate?'

Smith: 'Not from what I've been told.'

Wilkinson offered to come up again: 'I fucked around with you for a while and I apologise for that . . . I'm not interested in playing games anymore.'

Smith: 'Yeah, no worries.'

Then Wilkinson changed tack. 'Look,' he suddenly said, 'don't sit and think for one second Julie's entirely innocent . . . I'm going to press this as hard as I can . . . A couple of days after [I killed Kylie], I told Julie exactly what had happened. And it was Julie's idea that we say that it was Geoff Lowe . . . And the reason [was that I] don't believe by one second that she wasn't raped by Geoff Lowe . . . it was Julie's idea to blame Geoff Lowe.'

He referred to two other incidents where he claimed Julie had been badly treated by police officers and had not complained effectively. Then he said, 'I've said it to you before, Glenn. She was supposed to echo everything that I said.'

Smith: 'Yeah . . .'

Wilkinson: 'You know, I'm happy to do time for what I've done . . . and by rights I should. But, and I know it's taken a while for me to come clean with you, but she can't sit out there and say that she knew nothing, that's not right.'

Smith: 'Yeah . . .'

Wilkinson: 'I just want to make it clear to you, Glenn. Since I've been in here I've been finally getting medication.'

Smith: 'Yeah.'

Wilkinson: 'And obviously it's helping, if I'm sitting here and I'm talking to you decently. Whereas before I was a rude and arrogant little prick . . . so obviously we can get clearer lines of communication now . . .'

Smith: 'Yeah . . .'

Wilkinson: 'I'll keep on stressing it to you, Glenn, just please, please don't let Julie fucking pull the wool over your eyes. She's a master of it.'

A possible reason for this new anger with Julie emerged soon after, when Wilkinson said, 'My mother and father have been dragged through the Family Law Court . . . for access to Bradley . . . She's claiming my mother and father never had anything to do with Bradley. That's bullshit. You phone-tapped me all the time. Every morning she's ringing up [my parents, saying], "Can you take Bradley? Can you take Bradley? Can you take Bradley?" And she stands up in the fucking Family Law Court and says, "Oh, no, no, they didn't look after him." She's lied.'

(According to Julie, it was Wilkinson's parents who instigated the Family Law action, and she says she did not lie.)

Smith: 'Are your parents represented in the Family Law Court?'

Wilkinson: 'Oh yeah, they are, but legal minds are fucking weird . . . You cannot let her get away with it, that's all I ask of you, Glenn . . . You've high-tailed me for so long, please put some of that energy towards her.'

In court the next day, 17 October, Terry Healey confirmed that Wilkinson would plead guilty to manslaughter but not murder, on the grounds that he had killed Kylie because of provocation or substantial impairment of his responsibility, or both. John Kiely said the Crown would not accept this and the charge was still murder. Wilkinson refused to plead guilty to this, so a trial would be needed after all. A start date of 18 November was set.

Because he now admitted he'd killed Kylie, the trial would

be considerably shorter than previously envisaged. The only issue the jury would need to resolve would be the degree of Wilkinson's responsibility. This would require further reports from the psychiatrists, and these were called for. This time they would have to assess Wilkinson's state of mind on 28 April 2004.

Meanwhile, Wilkinson accompanied Glenn Smith and a large team to Mooney Mooney again on 21 October. Karool Road is a gravel track that runs for some kilometres along Mooney Mooney Creek. There are a few houses along the way but much of it is bush, with swampy ground and scrappy vegetation, including ferns and vines. The far side of the greenish river is largely bush, with the occasional mangrove. In general, the area is isolated and provides many places where a body might be buried without anyone noticing.

Wilkinson was taken to the site by Corrective Services' special-operations officers. Because of his stroppy behaviour on his last outing, they were in no mood for any of his nonsense and told him that if he tried to escape, they would shoot him. This seemed to calm him down. As the search began and Smith and he walked, he asked if the detective had had a chance to look into the matters he'd raised the other day. Smith told him he'd been busy organising the search: 'I've done what normally takes a week in a couple of days.' Wilkinson, as always, appeared to have absolutely no interest in the immense effort involved in the searches and began rambling yet again about Julie's supposed rape. After a while, he complained about some of the police he could see, and Smith said, 'We've got about nine detectives. We're supposed to have twenty, twenty-one, and we've got nine.'

He wasn't sure how long the officers from the Forensic Services Group could stay: 'I'm pushing the envelope now with them . . . they've said that they've been out here three times [already].'

The two men kept chatting. Wilkinson was in a fairly good mood today and Smith was keen to keep him talking in the hope he might provide some useful information. At one stage he said to the prisoner, 'While I think of it, just make sure you have a good check for ticks and leeches. I picked a tick up probably last Wednesday when we came up here and I didn't find it until Saturday, I was starting to feel a bit ill. I've still got the lump on my neck there . . . It's still sore.'

Wilkinson: 'You know they can't hurt you but.'

Smith: 'No, but they just make you feel a bit ordinary.'

Wilkinson: 'You got any, you know, these weeds called thistles?'

Smith: 'Yeah.'

Wilkinson: 'When you break the stem it's like a milky poison that comes out. You can get some of that and rub it on the, fuckin' where it was.'

Smith: 'Okay, I'll give it a run.'

Wilkinson identified a patch of bush in a fifty metre arc and Smith looked at it, saying, 'The bush is pretty thick, in four years it's grown, so it's hard to walk through. How deep did you bury the body?'

Wilkinson: 'I'd say about a foot.'

Smith: 'So not much soil on top?'

Wilkinson: 'I wouldn't even say a foot, though. I wouldn't even say a foot.'

Smith kept questioning Wilkinson, trying to get him to

recall the events of 28 April and be more specific about where the grave might be. One of the things in his mind was that Wilkinson was lazy. His history showed he didn't like physical exercise, or indeed effort of any kind. It was unlikely he would have taken Kylie far from the track or buried her deeply.

Wilkinson gave the appearance of trying to be helpful, saying, 'I'm more than happy to keep walking down the track. I don't want to get back into court and youse come in there and say, well, the barrister gets up, the prosecutor gets up and says, "Your Honour, we've looked but again—nothing."'

Smith: 'Um.'

Wilkinson: 'I don't want to have to go through that again.' Then he changed direction suddenly: 'What's the prosecutor reckon?'

Smith: 'How do you mean?'

Wilkinson: 'Well, in terms of length of sentence.'

Smith: 'He hasn't even spoken about that to us.'

Wilkinson: 'Why did he mention to Terry [Healey] thirty on the top and eighteen on the bottom?'

Smith: 'I can only guess. I wasn't present when that happened . . . Our barrister doesn't talk to me direct a great deal. When he gets questions in court he'll come and ask me, and we'll talk for a short time sometimes before court or sometimes just after. The rest of the time it's through the solicitor, Helen Rallis. I've not asked him about sentence . . . we're not even at that stage.'

Wilkinson: 'I'll probably get into shit for talking to you, but it's my life, I make the decisions for myself. You know, sixteen, fourteen, sixteen, it's not a problem. If youse come out to the jail tomorrow and say, "All right, we'll accept that," well, fuck, I'll take it . . . I just don't want to waste any more time, you know what I mean?'

Smith: 'Yeah.'

Wilkinson: 'Coz I'm sure you've got fuckin', plenty of other jobs to fuckin' do.'

Smith: 'I've just been concentrating on this one lately. It's keeping me more than busy.'

The detective tried to get more information from Wilkinson about the night of the murder. He said Kylie had left home with two suitcases but Wilkinson could remember only one. He asked what had happened to it, and Wilkinson said Julie had dumped it in the Georges River; he seemed determined to try to take Julie down with him.

More searches were conducted over the next few weeks. They involved the use of ground-penetrating radar, excavators and slashers, a cadaver dog, a boat and many police officers doing a line search at arm's length from each other, accompanied by an anthropologist and an archaeologist. On one weekend, Smith and another Gosford detective, Steve Norton, went to Karool Road on their own time and cleared some ground. Despite all this effort, no grave was found. Alan Wilkinson, whose house is fairly near the search sites, was not seen. The searchers did encounter funnelweb spiders, a diamond python, and various leeches and ticks. The cost of these latest efforts was $26,900.

★

Kylie's family was advised of each search before it occurred, and Carol was so anxious that she took time off work and sat by the phone at home. These experiences contributed to the depression she suffered for years after Kylie's disappearance. There were also more court hearings over various legal matters, all placing yet more pressure on the family.

On 12 November there was another surprise: Wilkinson changed his mind again and announced he was now prepared to plead guilty to murder. John Kiely, still wary about his unpredictability, asked Justice Johnson to formally convict the prisoner, and he did so. It was a dramatic moment.

Kylie's family were deeply affected, in some ways pleased but also bitter. Leanne realised that by avoiding a trial, Wilkinson would be able to keep many of his secrets and she would never learn much of what had happened in the last months of Kylie's life.

John had tears in his eyes, tears of hope that the court process was finally over. When the family left the courtroom, he felt dizzy and had trouble breathing. He sat down on a bench in the foyer and began to feel pains in his chest and a tingling in his fingers. Loosening his tie did not help and the pains got worse; he had to lie down. An ambulance was called and he was taken to St Vincent's Hospital. He was discharged later that day.

The next and final step in the state's judicial response to Kylie's murder was for Wilkinson to be sentenced. This is a two-part process. First there is a court hearing, at which the prosecution and defence barristers present submissions regarding an appropriate sentence. The prosecution usually includes victim impact statements, which in a murder case may be read aloud by members of the victim's family. The defence often presents statements from psychiatrists or psychologists seeking to explain the prisoner's actions. The judge then considers this and other relevant material, and about a month later there is another court appearance where the judge announces the sentence and the reasons for it.

Sentencing submissions for Wilkinson were due to be heard on 21 November. But first, he again said he wanted to help police find Kylie's grave. He again said he wanted to be interviewed by Glenn Smith. Again he was interviewed. And again, on 14 November, police returned to Mooney Mooney Creek for another search. Again Carol Edwards waited by the phone for a call from Smith to say whether her daughter's body had been found.

The site Wilkinson now identified was some six hundred metres from the previous one, along the same track. This time the cadaver dog expressed interest in a particular spot and returned to it later. The vegetation was cut down with a slasher, and an excavator was brought down the long track to dig the site. Several days later, the cadaver dog was brought back but no grave was found.

On 21 November, Wilkinson appeared in court, and yet again his barrister said he wanted to tell police where Kylie was buried, which was somewhere else along Mooney Mooney Creek. 'The prisoner instructs me this morning that he is prepared to go to the site with the police,' said Terry Healey. 'I know there's been some misinformation supplied in the past . . . He instructs me that if the cadaver dog was an efficient dog, he would have located the body of the deceased [already] . . . It would seem that every effort should be made in the interests of justice for the family of [Kylie] to locate her.'

John Kiely put Glenn Smith back in the witness box to confirm that Wilkinson had not indicated this new location on either of his two previous visits to Mooney Mooney with police. 'What's the attitude now of the police to attending the scene a third time with the prisoner?' he asked.

'I'm loath to do it,' said the detective, 'on account of the cost, both in time [and] organisation.' Kiely established that the searches so far had cost a bit over $119,000, and said to Smith, 'You of course would have to approach your senior officers to obtain permission for [another expensive search]?'

'I'm trying to think of a nice way to put it,' Smith replied. 'My name is not very good with the various sections involved . . . It would be problematic . . . to organise another one.'

Discussion turned to the two searches that had been conducted years earlier in the Royal National Park, and finally Smith stepped down to discuss the prospect of another search (which might delay sentencing) with Kylie's family. They gathered, with the lawyers, in a small room near the court.

There'd been much discussion among the detectives as to just what to make of Wilkinson's claims about the location of Kylie's grave. Was he simply lying or had he genuinely forgotten? Or had he had help in burying the body, which had later been moved without his knowledge? They decided it was likely he was simply lying. Homicide police have experience with being shown graves and know that their location is not something murderers forget. Usually, it is seared in their memory. Even if the body had been moved later by an accomplice, Wilkinson ought to have been more certain about where the original grave had been.

There were other reasons for thinking Wilkinson was playing games with them. He'd given two completely different general locations for the grave, the Royal National Park and Mooney Mooney. Obviously, at least one of them had to be wrong. But even at the Mooney Mooney Creek location, the places he'd indicated were several hundred metres or more from each other along a straight road marked with a very obvious landmark: the enormous bridge. Anyone who visits Karool Road can see that the potential for confusion on this scale is just not there.

Smith went over some of these matters with the family now. Michael had flown down from Singapore, so they were all there. Smith thought further searches would be a waste of time but he was prepared to abide by the family's decision.

John said, 'I don't want them to search again, I don't want to play his games anymore. He's pleaded guilty, let's draw a line in the sand and move on.'

The others agreed. They wanted Wilkinson sentenced as soon as possible.

When Smith returned to the witness box, Kiely said, '[The family have] expressed their opinion that [the searches have] gone on far enough?'

Smith: 'Yes.'

Kiely: 'That they had been traumatised by it as far as it has gone?'

Smith: 'Yes.'

Kiely: 'And as far as they're concerned, I think they want to draw a line in the sand and say "That's it"?'

Smith: 'That's correct.'

The family were sitting on the court benches with straight backs, mostly not touching each other. There was a tremendous sense of isolation and bleakness. It was a big decision they had just taken, and completely understandable. The wear and tear of the court process and the futile searches had been enormous. Michael had been appalled when he returned a week earlier and saw the emotional toll. Later he said, 'The week leading up to that hearing, being at home, I could see the family changing a bit as everybody prepared in their own way. After attending the hearing I was shocked. I don't know how my father, mother and sister could handle coming here week after week.'

The sentencing was further delayed for various technical reasons, including the difficulty the defence was having in obtaining a report from the psychiatrist Olav Nielssen. At a court hearing on 2 December, one of Kylie's cousins had an altercation with Wilkinson's mother outside the court. Fortunately, Glenn Smith came around the corner and got between the two women. When the court reconvened and the judge came in, Wilkinson said, 'Could I just say some thing, your honour?'

Johnson said, 'I suggest you don't say anything without speaking firstly to your counsel.'

'No, I'm going to say something,' said Wilkinson. 'I can well understand the family's got the shits with me, I can well understand that, but don't take it out on my mother, don't take it out on anyone else in the family. If you want to have a problem with me, have a problem with me.'

To which Johnson replied, 'Yes. Just have a seat, thank you, Mr Wilkinson.'

On the same day, during an adjournment, Wilkinson said he wanted to talk to Glenn Smith. Helen Rallis and Wilkinson's lawyers witnessed the conversation.

'At about 10.15 p.m. I phoned Alan about the body,' he said, presumably referring to 28 April 2004. 'But Alan has moved it on the left of the clearing on the left of the slope.'

'You mean your uncle Alan?' said Smith.

'Yeah . . . someone told me, but I'm not saying who, that Alan has gone back and moved the body.'

There is no evidence that Alan Wilkinson had any involvement in Kylie's death or in the disposal of her body.

Wilkinson asked Smith if he'd received a letter he'd sent him about Julie. Smith hadn't, but the letter turned up a few days later. It read: 'Detective Smith, Julie is involved much more than you realise.' It claimed Wilkinson had never taken her to an alleged gravesite in the Royal National Park. Most of the rest of the three-page letter consisted of ravings about the alleged rape of 2001. Like much else that Wilkinson said and wrote, it makes a layperson curious about how the psychiatrists found him sane.

★

At what was to have been a sentencing hearing on Monday 15 December, John Kiely stood up and announced yet another surprise. Wilkinson had sacked Terry Healey and Frances McGowan, the lawyers who'd been representing him for three and a half years.

McGowan had received a letter:

Dear Frances,

After an extended visit with family this morning I regret to inform yourself and Terry that I will be seeking further legal representation. I sincerely apologise for any inconvenience that this decision may have caused, my decision is based upon the family pressure I am currently experiencing. I wish to thank both of you for everything that you have done for me over the time.

Yours truly,

Paul James Wilkinson

PS Gaol is hard enough without family and friends continuously bombarding me at every given chance.

The new solicitor, Paul Donnelly, was in court. He had been hired two days earlier, and asked for an adjournment until Friday so he could bring himself up to date and hire a new barrister. Johnson, plainly concerned at the introduction of further delays—it was now two months since the trial had been due to begin—mentioned that the case 'already has a long history' and 'a change of legal representation at this stage has a significant impact upon the administration of justice. What do you expect to happen on the next occasion, the sentencing hearing to proceed?'

Donnelly had one more surprise for the court: 'My instructions are that he wishes to withdraw his plea of guilty.'

For a while there it had looked as though this stage of the suffering of Kylie's family was almost over. Now Paul Wilkinson had made everything uncertain once again.

THE MAN WHO TOLD STORIES

In order to change a plea from guilty to not guilty, you need to have a good reason. Wilkinson claimed he'd been duped into pleading guilty by false information from his lawyers. The only 'trial' Paul Wilkinson would ever have was about to begin, however it was not he who was being accused of anything but his barrister and solicitor. The six-day hearing that followed, spread over several months, was to expose details of the dealings between lawyers and client, something not often done because they are usually confidential, being protected by legal privilege.

In an affidavit, Wilkinson set out his argument, all of which was later denied by his former lawyers. He admitted giving police false statements about Kylie's grave and how she died: 'I did so at the time because I was deeply depressed and saw it as a form of retaliation against my aggressors.' He said his lawyers had told him there were to be 150 witnesses for the prosecution, and he didn't know who they would be or what they would say. He was depressed by this and 'decided to enter a plea of guilty to end it all . . . I was aware that any person who had been charged would receive reduced sentence if they entered a plea of guilty.' He had not been informed of the conclusions of the psychiatrists who had interviewed him, and if he had been aware of Olav Nielssen's original concerns about his fitness, 'I would not have entered a plea of guilty for murder or manslaughter'. He had been influenced to plead guilty because his barrister, Terry Healey, had said to him, 'Your sentence could be anywhere from sixteen years to eighteen years.' Wilkinson said, 'I thought about the length of the sentence and was of the opinion that I could serve such a sentence' [but not the longer one he now knew was standard]. Finally, he wrote, 'I state clearly that I did not kill Kylie Labouchardiere. I am not aware that she is dead and alternatively if she is dead I do not know where the body is currently located.'

It is unusual for someone to apply to reverse a plea, and Justice Johnson had to determine whether he had the right to consider such an application. He heard arguments on 19 December from a barrister hastily arranged by Wilkinson's new solicitor. The proceedings then ran into the courts' long Christmas break, and resumed on 29 January 2009 with another barrister, Robert Sutherland SC, who had been retained just two days earlier and had not had time to prepare properly. Sutherland, who was to take the matter through to the end, was a big man with a fleshy face and a short beard. His red and white reading glasses provided a touch of colour rarely seen at the Sydney bar.

The court sat that day in the King Street Courts. As always, there was a huge amount of paper. The judge had a revolving bookcase next to his chair, and before he appeared his associate brought out two thick binders full of laws and cases, several books and three thick ring-binders. John Kiely arrived dragging a small suitcase on wheels and carrying a large folder beneath his arm: the prosecution by now had ten thick white binders of documents, which had to be brought by Helen Rallis from the DPP's offices at the other end of the city. Wilkinson, as always, appeared in court in his prison greens. His little beard was gone.

Attending court continued to be deeply disturbing for Kylie's family. Leanne later recalled, 'I continually had to readjust my plans, like my roster at work and care of my children. I was torn between being at court for my sister and being a mother to my girls.' Her daughters had to deal with serious adult issues: 'Whenever I've been in court [and come home] they ask every time, "Was he there today?", "What did he look like?", "Did he say where Aunty is?" and "Did he say how he did it?"'

Carol suffered post-traumatic stress following Kylie's disappearance and was under the care of a psychologist. She took extensive periods off work and struggled financially during the long months of the court hearings.

Rebekkah Craig was keen to attend all the hearings. It's something police like to do when they've been involved in a long investigation, partly from the satisfaction and partly in case the lawyers need any information in a hurry. But the process was drawn out and she gave birth to her second child on 5 February, which marked the end of her attendances. In any case, she hadn't spent much time inside the court—Wilkinson noticed her there three or four times and demanded she leave. He had no right to do this but she left anyway, to avoid any outbursts from him. On those occasions she waited outside, and Smith would later tell her what had happened. It was yet another example of Wilkinson's efforts to retain some sort of control.

On 29 January and several other days over the next few months, the court sat to consider various technical matters. Sometimes the hearings were brief. Some of the professionals involved were frustrated by various aspects of the long-running case, even those who had come onto the scene more recently. On 31 March, solicitor Paul Donnelly, under pressure from the judge to speed things up, told him, 'I have seen Mr Wilkinson in total eighteen times, your honour, and on each of those occasions the instructions have varied greatly. It is very difficult to get reasonable instructions from him . . . His stories border on the sublime to the ridiculous. It just goes from one end of the spectrum to the other.' Donnelly's own performance was later criticised by the judge.

Johnson decided he did have the power to make a decision on Wilkinson's application to change his plea, and on 1 April 2009 he began to take arguments for and against it. This was three and a half months after Wilkinson had announced he was not guilty after all, a regrettably long time for the suffering of Kylie's family to be extended. There had been various reasons for this delay: nothing happens quickly in the courts, and when something unusual occurs, things slow down even more. The next day Johnson said, 'The way in which this application has proceeded now over months, ultimately doesn't show great credit on all involved, including, I suppose, myself for not more fiercely case-managing it.'

The problem was that Wilkinson was being dealt with by a system designed to protect the human rights of those caught up in it. Considerable amounts of time and money are spent to ensure a fair outcome, even when this involves a delay in the judicial process because of some unusual or even unreasonable action by the accused. This is the price of justice, and most of us accept that it is worth paying.

But there is an assumption the number of such delays will be small in any one case. Wilkinson, with all his lies and changes of mind, introduced far more delays than is normal, and the system is not designed to respond to this. It plodded on, without taking into account the cumulative effect of what Wilkinson was doing, in the same way the police complaints system had plodded on in the case of Geoff Lowe.

One person who was no longer in court was John Edwards. After stopping work in mid-2008, he'd gone to Thailand a few times with Michael. They visited the sights, and also sat and talked. It was a valuable experience: John realised, after collapsing outside the court back in Sydney, that he had been alone with his emotions for too long. On one of his trips with Michael, his son told him about the new lease of life he'd found in Asia. 'Dad,' he said, 'when you go back to Australia, you'll hate it.'

Michael took him for a ride up one of the rivers in a long boat, and it brought back memories of the time John had spent in Asia when he was a young man in the army, a happy time. He started to cry, realising he'd forgotten how simple life could be, and thought, 'I need this. This is where I really need to be.'

When he reached Sydney Airport after one of these trips, John went through Customs and was waiting to collect his bag. He looked around and saw aggression everywhere, in the way people were standing and speaking, even in the way they looked at each other. He thought, 'This is dog-eat-dog—there's no respect for anyone here. In Thailand, they all respect one another. If someone falls over in the street, three or four people will go and pick you up. In Australia, they'll kick you to see if you're still alive.' And there was, of course, the fact that Kylie lay somewhere in its soil, in an unmarked grave. That continued to tear at his heart, and while he was in Australia he would always be thinking of little else. In January 2009 he moved to Thailand.

The case wore on, now in Court Five on the St James side of the old court complex, with the judge and the barristers in their yellowed wigs and their gowns. At times it seemed as though it might continue forever. Carol Edwards noted bitterly that Wilkinson himself, whose changes of plea were largely responsible for the absurd length of the proceedings, didn't appear in the witness box once. His affidavits (there were two of them now), containing his claims as to why he had pleaded guilty, had been received by the court on the assumption he would be cross-examined over them. Surely this ought to have been a requirement, given that the court had taken his change of mind and his allegations against his lawyers so seriously. But legally it wasn't compulsory, and the only people who did go into the box were the two psychiatrists, Olav Nielssen and Stephen Allnutt, and Wilkinson's sacked lawyers, Terry Healey and Frances McGowan.

The legal point being considered was not Wilkinson's guilt but the integrity of his plea of guilty. There were two broad issues to be determined: whether he had been mentally fit enough to make the decision, and whether, as he claimed, his lawyers had misled him on some of the relevant facts.

The psychiatrists disagreed on whether Wilkinson had been fit to plead. Stephen Allnutt, for the prosecution, was an older man, balding and with a big head. He spoke carefully and sometimes licked a finger before turning a page of his notes. He had interviewed Wilkinson several times, including on 10 November, the day Wilkinson had given signed instructions to his lawyers to enter a plea of guilty, and was in no doubt about his fitness.

Olav Nielssen, on the other hand, had provided a report on 30 January saying that responses in the interview he'd conducted with Wilkinson on 6 November 'raise significant concerns about his fitness to enter a plea and his fitness for trial'. Nielssen was much younger than Allnutt, a keen man with short, sandy hair and glasses, who appeared to be chewing gum while under cross-examination. He said it had not always been easy to assess Wilkinson's state of mind: 'I should probably describe how unusual Mr Wilkinson is to interview . . . [He] is one of the very unusual people that I have had the opportunity to interview on three occasions and I have not been certain as to what is wrong with him. I am guessing that there is an underlying psychotic illness but it is a guess, because I don't know if he is pulling my leg or not half the time. That's the fact of the matter.'

It was nice to hear that Wilkinson had managed to puzzle an expert, as well as just about every one else he'd had dealings with.

Wilkinson himself spoke in court only once during the six days of this hearing. John Kiely had just asked Nielssen why he'd described Wilkinson's original explanation of Kylie's death as 'bizarre', and the psychiatrist said it was bizarre 'when you put it in its context with all the other crimes he claimed were related to this event. For example, the missing rocket-launchers.'

At this point, Wilkinson said from the dock, 'I'm not going to sit through this.'

'Please sit quietly, Mr Wilkinson,' said the judge.

And he did.

John Kiely asked Nielssen, 'There was no other psychiatric tool you could hang anything on, other than these bizarre beliefs, that led you to the belief that he was unfit to plead. Is that right?'

Nielssen: 'Yes, and they are presented in such a way, I almost wondered if he was pulling my leg. I did ask him that: "Are you just pulling my leg?"'

Kiely: 'You have heard me quote from Dr Allnutt's report that [Wilkinson] was not being honest with the forensic psychiatrists. Did you think for one moment that he might have been swinging the lead, so to speak, to try and get into this position?'

Nielssen: 'Yes, I certainly considered that. That is apparent in my conclusion, the difficulty I had in reaching a firm opinion.'

When Allnutt gave evidence, he noted that Wilkinson had actually told a prison psychiatrist who was treating him that he had not been open with the forensic psychiatrist (that is, Allnutt himself or perhaps Nielssen). Allnutt recounted how Wilkinson had talked to him about hearing voices.

Kiely: 'Did that cause you to have any suspicion about the validity of his claim?'

Allnutt: 'Yes, it did.'

Kiely: 'In what way, doctor?'

Allnutt: '. . . he didn't appear to be able to spontaneously describe those experiences to me and that was on both occasions that I interviewed him [on 10 November and 20 February] . . . I got the impression that he couldn't find words to describe it. And most people who have true auditory hallucinations, especially for the length of time he describes them, would have no difficulty in describing those experiences. So that was the one thing. The other thing was that I thought there were some atypical aspects to the voice in particular on that occasion . . . I asked him whether or not he heard the voices in stereo or in one ear or the other, and he answered "One ear", which is a highly atypical way of experiencing voices, in one ear. I found him to be relatively evasive when I started challenging him in regard to that, so at that stage I was sceptical.'

Allnutt's view of Wilkinson after last interviewing him

had been that 'some of his answers appear to be part of a deliberate attempt to confuse the interviewer', so that 'whether or not he suffers a mental illness is in question'.

In conclusion, Allnut continued, 'While I accept that he likely has in the past and could currently suffer depression and anxiety symptoms, I am less sure that he suffers active symptoms of psychosis; and [at] this stage I would defer making a diagnosis of psychosis.'

In their attempt to reject Allnutt's opinion, the defence was relying on the report it had requested from Nielssen and obtained on 30 January 2009, which said briefly that Wilkinson had not been fit to plead back in November. The problem with this was that, as we have seen, on 13 October Nielssen had found him fit to be tried, and there was no record of any subsequent deterioration of his mental state.

Nielssen said he had interviewed Wilkinson again on 6 November 2008 and changed his mind. But with further questioning by Kiely, it emerged there was no indication of this in his notes of that interview, which actually recorded that Wilkinson's condition had *improved*. There was also the question of why, if Nielssen had changed his mind about Wilkinson's fitness on 6 November, he hadn't communicated this to Wilkinson's lawyers, given the guilty plea that was made less than a week later. These were serious matters.

Questioned by Justice Johnson, Nielssen agreed that the Expert's Code of Conduct for the state of New South Wales places certain obligations on someone in his position. These include 'an overriding duty to assist the Court impartially on matters relevant to the expert witness's area of expertise'. He acknowledged that the failure to advise Wilkinson's lawyers, or the Court, of his lack of fitness to plead back in November had been 'a failing in my duties in that regard, your Honour'.

In the decision he later handed down, Justice Johnson said he did not accept that Nielssen had really believed there were serious concerns about Wilkinson's fitness at the interview of 6 November: 'In my view, a proper understanding of the concluding sentence in Dr Nielssen's report of 30 January [saying Wilkinson had not been fit to plead] is a form of after-the-event gloss which Dr Nielssen has placed upon earlier events.'

Once the issue of Wilkinson's sanity had been thrashed out by the psychiatrists, his former lawyers were interviewed regarding his claims that they'd misled him. The first in the box was solicitor Frances McGowan. Wilkinson's usual manner in court was to lean forward in the dock and stare at the low wall in front of him. Occasionally he would look around the courtroom with a faintly supercilious grin. But as McGowan gave evidence he sat straight and stared at her steadily. John Kiely asked her about Wilkinson's claim that Healey and she had been to see him on only three occasions from the time of his arrest to the time the matter had been set down for trial: 'What do you say about that, ma'am?'

She replied, 'It's incorrect. It is nonsense,' adding that there would have been at least ten visits. Asked by Robert Sutherland about the importance of Wilkinson's concern for his family in his decision to change his plea to guilty, she said, 'That was at the end [of his reasons], right at the end.'

Sutherland: 'What other reasons did he give?'

McGowan: 'Well, that he did it. He said, "I did it."'

Her evidence over, McGowan left the courtroom, stared

at by Wilkinson's mother and four supporters who were there. One was the skinny Aboriginal woman, today wearing a top on which masking tape spelled out the words 'MIN NO NIGGER'.

Wilkinson's mum still looked angry, maybe scared. In one of the breaks she complained to her son's solicitor, 'You can't hear a flipping thing in there. The only time they talk loud is when they want to talk about Paul.'

The hearing dragged on, day after day, and some of those involved seemed increasingly edgy. Glenn Smith had postponed his sergeant's exam twice because of the prolonged court process: the case was now affecting his career. But he had to be there; the case had been part of his life for so long. Everyone was wondering whether Wilkinson would go into the witness box. The decision was his, and apparently he'd changed his mind several times. Most recently, he'd said he wouldn't be cross-examined. As he was the one who had to convince the court to allow him to withdraw his plea, this would do him no favours.

Barrister Terry Healey was cross-examined, particularly in regard to Wilkinson's claim that he had said the sentence would be between sixteen and eighteen years (rather than longer). He was an impressive witness, his answers prompt and definite.

Kiely: 'Did you say that to him?'

Healey, an older man with a beard and glasses, said, 'No, I didn't. In fact, they were Paul's words. As I recall it, he said, "You can tell that Glenn Smith if he wants the body then I expect I should get only sixteen to eighteen years" and I said to him, "You can't bind the Crown with that sort of thing,

Paul. What I told you about the twenty-five years [as a mini-mum] is more likely to be the case if you recover the body." '

Healey was asked about his notes of his meetings with Wilkinson, which contain some curious passages. Here is one from 2 December 2008: 'Paul initially instructed us this morning that his uncle Alan was present when an argument ensued between his uncle and Kylie. His uncle strangled Kylie . . . Paul and his uncle then buried the body near Mooney Mooney Creek . . . The shovel used was Uncle Alan's.'

Wilkinson later said 'he was responsible for Kylie's death and that Uncle Alan only helped bury her with his shovel. Paul went back the following week . . . with Uncle Alan and they inspected the burial site together'. Later, 'Paul informed us that he had been informed on the weekend from members of his family that the reasons for lack of recovery of the body where Paul insists she is buried is due to the fact that Uncle Alan has told Paul's direct family that he had removed the body and buried it elsewhere'. At the end of this record of interview, Healey had noted, 'Really do not know what to believe.'

As previously noted, there is no evidence connecting Alan Wilkinson to Kylie's murder. Nor is there evidence linking any member of the Wilkinson family to knowledge of the disposal of Kylie's body.

On one occasion, Healey even visited Mooney Mooney Creek himself to look for the grave at a location identified by Wilkinson. This is not the sort of thing barristers normally do; presumably, he was becoming frustrated. After failing to find the grave, he tried to have a conversation about this with Wilkinson, who refused to talk about it. Healey didn't say this in court, but Wilkinson must have been the client from hell. Healey was asked, as McGowan had been, to recall the conversation on 4 November in which Wilkinson had said he would plead guilty to killing Kylie.

'He didn't want to cause his family, his parents, the stress of going to trial,' the barrister recalled, 'and his words were, "Well, I killed her, I murdered her. I am pleading guilty to murder."' The following conversation had then occurred.

Healey: 'Do you really mean that, Paul?'

Wilkinson: 'Yes.'

Healey: 'Do you understand the implications of what you have just said?'

Wilkinson: 'Yes.'

Healey: 'That you deliberately murdered her.'

Wilkinson: 'Yes.'

In the dock, Wilkinson, who for today's appearance had shaved his head, listened impassively. Maybe he didn't realise how bad all this made him look. Or maybe he was just happy people were still talking about him. It's not as though he or his family were paying: his defence was funded from the public purse.

Later, Sutherland told the court, 'I had intended to call my client. My instructions today are that he does not wish to give evidence. I have explained to him the effect that will have on the weight the tribunal will give to the assertions in that affidavit.'

Wilkinson kept staring at the front of the dock. As always, he had avoided direct confrontation with people in authority. He might hate them but he could never deal with them.

★

Justice Johnson was to give his big decision on 21 April 2009. Would Wilkinson go to trial or was he guilty once and for all of the murder of Kylie Labouchardiere?

The judge was a few minutes late coming into court and the lawyers chatted among themselves, more relaxed than previously; their work was done, at least for the moment. Some of the other detectives who'd worked the case had turned up in their dark suits and sat with Glenn Smith. John and Michael Edwards weren't there: they were out of the country.

Carol and Leanne were sitting on the hard wooden benches, with relatives who'd come along to support them. A female Salvation Army officer sat next to Carol, trying to comfort her by patting her leg. Wilkinson's family was there too. Five court marshals were present in case of trouble, with four standing at the rail dividing the public gallery from the rest of the room.

There were few journalists present. Because of the prolonged nature of the proceedings, and a suppression order that had been placed on coverage for a long time while the searches for Kylie's grave occurred, the media had largely forgotten about the case.

There was the sudden customary knock on the door to one side of the judge's chair and Justice Johnson came striding in, wearing wig and gown, his head bowed and some legal texts clasped under one arm. He sat and abruptly started to read his judgement, going through the psychiatric evidence and concluding that Wilkinson had been mentally fit to plead guilty.

One reason for this was that the defence had asked another

psychiatrist, Bruce Westmore, to examine Wilkinson on 31 March 2009, and he had concurred with Allnutt's view. Johnson noted that 'The various psychiatrists who have examined [Wilkinson] have referred to his evasiveness and propensity to make misleading statements in various respects. There is a live debate as to whether the applicant suffers from any psychotic disorder.'

He then turned to the question of why Wilkinson had pleaded guilty to murder, and said he was satisfied he did so 'in the face of a very strong circumstantial case against him, and in circumstances where he believed that such an approach would operate to his advantage on sentence.'

This was not uncommon and provided no basis for a grant of leave for Wilkinson to withdraw his plea. Johnson determined that, on the whole, Wilkinson had been well served by his lawyers. He noted that he had changed his plea twice (from not guilty to guilty and back to not guilty), which did not help his case, and concluded: 'The applicant has failed to establish that the plea of guilty to murder was not really attributable to a consciousness of guilt.'

The application to withdraw the plea was rejected: Paul Wilkinson was (still) guilty of murder. There was a gasp from Carol but nothing more: she seemed stunned. Wilkinson, staring down for most of the judge's speech, looked up as he announced his decision. He had already told Sutherland that he would appeal such an outcome, and now, after a fleeting expression of anguish crossed his face, he entered into an animated conversation with his lawyers. Maybe he was still trying to kid himself that he had some kind of control.

They asked for a brief adjournment, and Sutherland spoke

to Kiely and Rallis, who then took Carol and Leanne aside. Yet again, Wilkinson was offering to reveal where Kylie was buried.

Carol said to Leanne, 'How can we change our decision when half the family's overseas and can't be involved? We can't do that.'

She told the lawyers the earlier family decision still stood, and everyone went back into court, where Wilkinson was told the news.

'He slumped,' Carol later recalled, 'he was like a broken person. I looked at him and thought, "I've cut the power. He doesn't have that hold over this family anymore. I've cut it."'

Sutherland asked for an adjournment until another day to prepare further for the sentencing process, and Johnson refused. This case had gone on long enough.

SENTENCE

When deciding how long a convicted person should go to jail, a judge is required to consider various guidelines, including mandatory minimum penalties and previous sentences given for the same offence. The judge must take into account aspects of the case that might reduce the sentence, including any discount to be given for a guilty plea and any remorse shown by the prisoner. The prosecution and the defence barristers make oral and written submissions on these and other matters during a sentencing hearing, which takes place in open court and typically lasts for up to a few hours.

Another element in these hearings is the reading of victim impact statements, by those who were close to the person who was killed. The terrible effect of the crime on these people, usually family members, is now acknowledged in the judicial system by the term used to describe them: 'secondary victims'.

So it was that on 21 April 2009, soon after Justice Johnson had rejected Wilkinson's attempt to reverse his plea, Leanne Edwards was called to the witness box to read the statement she'd prepared. She spoke in a soft voice, on the verge of tears but becoming more confident as she went on. She recalled the confusion of the first week after Kylie's disappearance, when no one had any idea what had happened. Then came the need to try to explain to her daughters, aged four and seven, why their aunty had gone away.

Three years later, when Paul Wilkinson was charged, 'All hope of seeing her, hearing her and speaking to her again, everything was gone forever.' Wilkinson, she said, 'has robbed me of us growing together as sisters by spending quality time together—like going shopping or going out to watch a girly movie. [He] has robbed me of being an aunty in the future and us sharing experiences as mothers. [He] has robbed me of being able to celebrate with my sister all special occasions, Christmas, birthdays, achievements made by her nieces, and all family gatherings.'

Carol Edwards wrote (her statement was read for her) that Kylie's disappearance had aged her own mother, Louisa Windeyer, twenty years and affected her health, thereby 'doubling the pressure I have been under with the worry of her wellbeing . . . It has been a living nightmare for myself and my family since Paul Wilkinson was arrested as Kylie's alleged killer eighteen months ago. My daughter Leanne and I have attended each and every court session, and every time feel more despair as he fails to reveal the whereabouts of her remains. He continues to play these games at the family's expense . . . Whatever sentence is given to Paul Wilkinson for murdering my daughter will never compare with the life sentence of grief he has given to me and her extended family.'

Statements from John and Michael were read out by members of the Homicide Victims Support Group. John, after recording the disintegration of his life, wrote: 'I am no longer the same person I was when Kylie was alive.'

Paul Wilkinson leaned slightly forwards during these statements and stared straight ahead, a half-smile occasionally on his lips. It was as though he had no idea of the seriousness of what was being said. Never had the gap between him and other people seemed greater. Carol glanced at the back of his head and thought about the knowledge stored there that might have been such a comfort to the family, had he chosen to reveal it.

After the victim impact statements, John Kiely said some words in support of a fourteen-page written submission he'd given the judge. It was his last contribution to the matter. He summarised the Crown's argument that Wilkinson had killed Kylie because he feared their relationship (and Kylie's pregnancy) was about to become known to Julie, and that this would destroy his marriage, which he wanted to preserve. The Crown submitted that 'the prisoner has been guilty of conduct so reprehensible that the only sentence appropriate in this case is that of a life sentence'.

John Kiely said that the absence of information about Kylie's last moments made things worse.

'That,' he said, 'is what makes this case so difficult and so evil, in my submission, because . . . we will never know, no one will ever know how she died, where she died, or what happened to her.' But we can speculate, he noted, based on what Wilkinson had said about her death, and such speculation is not pleasant.

He summarised the macabre story Wilkinson had told the Police Integrity Commission. 'The situation then is this,' he continued. 'The family have that knowledge [of what Wilkinson told the PIC] and they are left with the situation of: I wonder if Kylie died this way? I wonder if that was what really happened and he was responsible and he did these things and he is the one now making the allegations that it was police officer Lowe who did it. It is often said that the worst thing in life is not knowing.'

It was a terrible thought but it had to be expressed, even if it presented the worst imaginable scenario. Anyone familiar with Wilkinson's ravings in the year before he was arrested must have wondered if some of his stories about Geoff Lowe's murder of Kylie were efforts to transfer his own guilt. 'Call me cruel,' Wilkinson had written to Julie a long time ago, in the privacy of a text message. Now a Crown prosecutor was suggesting that's exactly what he was, in an open court. And he was basing that suggestion on Wilkinson's own words.

On the defence side, affidavits were presented from Wilkinson's parents. His father, Ron, said Paul had never been in serious trouble before, but his life had changed after being stabbed in the stomach with a syringe at work: 'his circle of friends had grown smaller and he seemed continually worried . . . In my view he went through hell . . . At the time of my son's arrest I was extremely surprised, as it never occurred to me that my son could hurt anybody. Since his arrest, my wife and I have visited our son twice a week. I have noticed that he has become very withdrawn and he is not himself.'

Robert Sutherland argued that a life sentence was not appropriate precisely because nothing was known for sure about how Kylie had been killed: 'It's difficult to see how one can cherry-pick through various assertions by Mr Wilkinson over the various passages of time in order to buttress one conclusion rather than another.' His lack of remorse, demonstrated by his refusal to say where the grave was, was relevant to the length of the sentence but had no bearing on the seriousness of the crime that had preceded it. That was simply unknown.

Justice Johnson went away to consider all this. He was to deliver his sentence on 22 May. The day before this, Carol Edwards went into a church and lit a candle for Kylie. That night she found another candle at home, one that Kylie had given her, and she lit that too. It shone through the night and she thought about her lost daughter.

She wondered if the family had made the right decision the previous November, when they told Glenn Smith they didn't want any more searches. It was a decision Carol had thought about every day since. That night, she told herself they'd done the right thing. Kylie was with God now—it was only her bones that were in the ground. At least the family was no longer in the power of Paul Wilkinson.

Kylie had given her the candle the Christmas before she'd disappeared, and now Carol read the card that had come with it and thought about tomorrow. Part of her felt terrible for what had happened to Kylie: she'd made some stupid mistakes in her own life, and when Kylie went missing they'd come back to haunt her. She felt deeply guilty about the decision she'd made years before to leave her children for Robert McCann. If she hadn't done that, she thought, Kylie would have grown up differently. She might still be alive.

The previous day, Carol had spent an hour with her psychologist, who'd wanted to see her before the sentencing. John had flown in from Thailand and spent a day reading the Crown's statement of facts at the DPP's office, learning for the first time many of the details of Kylie's life in the months before her death. Michael could not be there: he was in Singapore, responsible for the installation of 6000 security cameras in a casino that was opening later that year.

Carol was very nervous about the judge's decision: as far as she was concerned, he was going to say what her girl's life had been worth. She knew Wilkinson wouldn't get life, but he might get thirty years. He deserved it: he hadn't just killed her daughter, he'd killed her grandchild too.

The sentence was handed down at the old sandstone Supreme Court building in Darlinghurst. Unlike the brick court complex in the city, this one has a large forecourt, with plenty of room for crowd control and the media. By now the case was attracting a lot of attention. Court Five was almost full with marshals, police, reporters, members of both families and some court watchers. John Edwards was no longer in the suit and tie he'd worn in court last year: he was tanned again and wearing a black, open-necked Thai suit.

Wilkinson was brought from prison in a van and put into one of the holding cells in the labyrinth of corridors beneath the building. The cells are dim places, with red bars and wooden benches. The corridors have concrete floors, low ceilings, flaking paint and hazard alarm buttons every few metres along the walls. Finally, Wilkinson, wearing his prison greens and white sandshoes, was brought up the steep narrow stairs leading directly into the dock. He chatted to his solicitor while they waited for the judge.

Johnson strode in, sat down and immediately began to read: 'On 28 April 2004, Kylie Labouchardiere set off on a journey to meet the offender, Paul James Wilkinson.'

He read well, with more volume and emphasis than usual. He took his audience on a journey too, into a relationship that had really started when Kylie and Wilkinson became acquainted at Sutherland Hospital in December 2003: 'I am satisfied that she responded positively, enthusiastically and happily to the developing relationship.' Between 21 December 2003 and 28 April 2004, he noted, the couple exchanged 23,836 phone calls and text messages.

'I am satisfied,' said Johnson, after referring to the text message discovered by Glenn Smith in which Wilkinson said they would be in Dubbo together, 'that Ms Labouchardiere and the offender made plans that he would leave his wife and child and move to Dubbo to take up a new life with Ms Labouchardiere . . . [But] when the offender set out to meet Ms Labouchardiere on 28 April 2004, he had no intention of leaving his wife and son to set up a new life with the victim. As with his approach to the female police officer in 2003, the offender was content to maintain a sexual relationship with

Ms Labouchardiere while maintaining his marriage. However, he had lied to Ms Labouchardiere that he was prepared to leave his wife. The position was further complicated by the victim's pregnancy to him.

'Although I do not think that the evidence permits a finding beyond reasonable doubt that the offender set out to meet the victim with the intention of killing her and disposing of her body, I am satisfied on the criminal standard that the offender realised that stern action would need to be taken by him to ensure that the victim did not cause him harm by informing others, especially his wife, of the relationship which had resulted in pregnancy.'

Johnson was satisfied Wilkinson had killed Kylie, but was not prepared to accept the account in his confession that he had strangled her. Wilkinson, he noted, 'has demonstrated an extensive history of deception, motivated by self-interest, over a number of years.' He referred to the text message in which Wilkinson had mentioned a weapon, and said he thought Wilkinson had not revealed the whereabouts of the body 'as he does not perceive it to be in his interests to do so'.

At first Wilkinson stared at the judge as he read the judgment, but Johnson did not see him: he did not look up once in the first twenty minutes.

On the public benches, Kylie's family listened, blank-faced. At one point, Wilkinson scratched 'PW 09' into the heavy varnish covering the wooden dock just in front of him. For most of the last fifteen minutes of the judgement, he looked around. Johnson said he did not think the murder was in the worst-case category, but it did lie 'clearly above the middle of the range of objective seriousness for the crime of murder'.

The standard non-parole (that is, minimum) sentence for murder is twenty years; the maximum is life. He sentenced Wilkinson to twenty-eight years, with a non-parole period of twenty-one years.

Wilkinson was not looking around now but stared down at the front of the dock. Johnson turned to the second charge, of setting alight the house at Picnic Point. He said it had been done for the purpose of covering up the murder, which placed it towards the top of the range of objective seriousness for this offence, for which the maximum penalty is imprisonment for ten years. He sentenced Wilkinson to six years, with a non-parole period of four and a half. Some but not all of the two sentences would be served concurrently. In total, Johnson concluded, Wilkinson was to serve a minimum of twenty-four years in jail, held to have begun when he was arrested on 17 April 2007. The earliest date on which Paul Wilkinson can leave prison is 16 April 2031.

Kylie's family had listened for over forty minutes without showing emotion. As the judge stood up and left the room, they began to weep.

AFTERWORD

Rebekkah Craig still works at Gosford and is busily raising the two children born during the investigation.

Glenn Smith returned to the Homicide Squad and received a Commander's Unit Citation for bringing Kylie's killer to justice. In order to become a sergeant he had to leave Homicide and now works in uniform at a suburban police station. He's proud of Paul Wilkinson's conviction but says, 'There are no winners in a murder investigation.'

Four days after Wilkinson was sentenced, Geoff Lowe applied to be classified 'hurt on duty' and given a pension for life, due to the psychological effects of Wilkinson's allegations. This was granted in 2010.

Julie Thurecht is engaged to Vince Cotton and living happily with him and Bradley.

John Edwards taught English in a high school in Thailand for several years and now helps provide first-aid courses in

Afghanistan. He still finds it immensely hard to talk about his younger daughter.

Leanne Edwards is a single parent, bringing up her daughters on the Central Coast. She believes Kylie was finally starting to mature just before her death, and if she'd lived her life would have improved dramatically. She thinks often about the way her own family's life would have been enriched had Kylie and her children been part of it, and of how Kylie and she might have grown close for the first time. 'I was waiting for her to catch up with me,' she says, 'and she just had when we lost her.'

Carol Edwards (nee Windeyer) believes Kylie is still close to her: 'I know that she's with me. I speak to her every day, out loud, when I'm walking to the station at three, three-thirty in the morning [to go to work at a call centre in Sydney]. There's a star just directly out there, it's the brightest star in the whole sky. I named this star Kylie. And this star follows me, all the way to the station, and I talk to this star. When I'm feeling down, I just speak out loud to her, it's as though she was here. I'm sure she's had a hand in some things that have happened to me since she died. I'm sure she's like a guardian angel watching over me.'

AUTHOR'S NOTE

A copy of the manuscript of this book was sent to Paul Wilkinson's parents in case he or they wished to read it and comment. I was told the family does not wish to add anything to what is on the public record.

THANKS

My heartfelt thanks to John and Carol Edwards, for their help and for various documents and photographs. I would not have written the book without their agreement, and hope the result warrants the anguish caused by recalling Kylie's life.

I owe a lot to many other people, and two in particular. The first is Anna Cooper, media officer for the NSW Director of Public Prosecutions. Most people in her position say no to anything unusual, but she said yes to the idea for this book and so did her boss at the time, Director of Public Prosecutions Nicholas Cowdery.

My other great debt is to Glenn Smith, the leader of the investigation that brought Paul Wilkinson to justice. Again, most people in his job are suspicious of journalists, but he was prepared over time to tell me a great deal about the investigation. My thanks to him, and to his bosses, who in the end let him talk on the record.

Thanks also to Julie and Jenene Thurecht, Geoff Lowe, Rebekkah Craig, Sean Labouchardiere, Leanne and Michael Edwards, John Kiely, Helen Rallis, Sue Lowe, Maxine Cahill, and others who spoke with me on condition of anonymity. My then editor, Peter Fray, enabled me to cover the case for the *Sydney Morning Herald*, and Justice Peter Johnson permitted access to documents presented to the court hearings.

Some of the above people read all or part of the manuscript of this book and provided helpful comments and corrections.

My final thanks are to book editor Catherine Milne, and to my wife, Alex Snellgrove, for many valuable suggestions, and to Jane Palfreyman, Elizabeth Cowell and Margaret Connolly.

INDEX

Michael Duffy

THE TOWER

Young detective Nicholas Troy is basically a good man, for whom working in homicide is the highest form of police work. But when a woman falls from the construction site of the world's tallest skyscraper, the tortured course of the murder investigation that follows threatens his vocation.

Hampered by politicised managers and incompetent colleagues, Troy fights his way through worlds of wealth and poverty, people smuggling and prostitution. He has always seen Sydney as a city of sharks, a place where predators lurk beneath the glittering surface. Now he uncovers networks of crime and corruption that pollute the city, reaching into the police force itself.

Finally, the shadowy predator Troy has been chasing turns and comes for him, putting his family at risk. Forced to defend himself with actions he would never have considered before, Troy confronts a moral abyss. He realises it's a long way down . . .

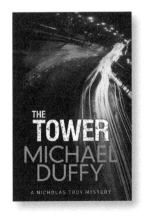

'A gripping, fast-paced debut that introduces Michael Duffy's simple, true and confident voice to an army of crime lovers. Sure to be a hit with fans of *Underbelly* and Michael Connelly, *The Tower* unites classic noir suspense with seat of the pants action set against the glimmer and grime of the harbour city, where the sharks are beginning to circle.'

SydneyUnleashed.com

ISBN 978 1 74237 261 7

Michael Duffy

THE SIMPLE DEATH

A man has come off the Manly Ferry and Detective Nicholas Troy investigates but he is distracted. His mentor Father Luke Corelli has been accused of abusing a young boy years before. To Troy's dismay he's not denying the charge and nor is the Catholic Church trying to defend his name. Troy's ambitious and attractive colleague Susan Conti is newly single and his eccentric boss, Jon McIver, would rather be singing the blues than following leads.

In another part of Sydney, successful bureaucrat Leila Scott's mother has bone cancer. She asks for help to die and Leila seeks the advice of a voluntary euthanasia group. She finds herself caught up in a police investigation when Troy comes across members of the group and begins to suspect voluntary euthanasia is being used as an excuse for something much darker.

As Troy digs deeper into both cases, feeling instinctively that they are somehow connected, he realises that morality and the law might not always follow the same path. And that there is no such thing as a simple death.

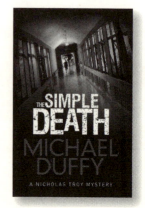

'Duffy is indisputably a writer to watch. He will soon be ranked alongside the likes of international behemoths Michael Connelly, George Pelecanos and Don Winslow. There is no higher praise.'

Winsor Dobbin, *Sun-Herald*

ISBN 978 1 74237 552 6